GW00771286

# How To
# Chat-up
# Women

## Matt Mountebank

SUMMERSDALE

Copyright © Summersdale Publishers 1994

All rights reserved.

No part of this book may be reproduced by any means, nor transmitted, nor translated into a machine language, without the written permission of the publisher.

Summersdale Publishers
PO Box 49
Chichester
PO19 2FJ
United Kingdom

A CIP catalogue record for this book is available from the British Library.

Printed and bound in Great Britain by Biddles Ltd., Guildford and Kings Lynn.

ISBN 1 873475 20 9

Original illustrations by Amanda Byfield.

# Important note:

*This book is about communicating with women in such a way that they find you attractive (the terms 'woman' and 'girl' in this book are interchangeable). None of the techniques outlined, however, can be a guarantee of success with any individual. They can only serve to point you in the right direction and hopefully enable you to avoid making mistakes. Remember at all times that a woman is never obliged to respond positively to your approaches. Always respect her right to say no, and always give her the opportunity to say so. While the tone of this manual is often light-hearted when referring to women, it does not mean that you should forget that they have feelings. Be bold in your chatting-up, but always temper that boldness with respect.*

# Contents

## SCENARIOS

# Introduction

*Men and women*
Men and women have lived together on this planet for thousands of years, but widespread lack of understanding between the sexes has long been a major cause of disharmony.

Think about the differences between men and women: there are the anatomical ones which enable women to go through the experience of pregnancy and to have children. There is the fact that women have a menstrual cycle that can alter their mood instantly. Then there are the 'artificial' divisions resulting from sexual conditioning that begins at birth and continues throughout life.

These artificial factors start with the most basic things such as dolls, pink clothes, and long hair for girls; toy cars, blue clothes and short hair for boys. At school, girls and boys are taught subjects deemed to be more suitable to one sex than to the other (eg. cookery for girls, metalwork for boys). In this 'enlightened' age, sexual stereotyping such as this is becoming less prevalent, but many of the adult women whom you will encounter will have been brought up to believe in the importance of acting in a manner that is 'ladylike' or feminine rather than simply being themselves. This heightens the sexual differences and the need for greater understanding on the part of the male.

Men are just as conditioned to their own sex as are women. Put yourself in their shoes for a moment: most women would wonder why so many men are fascinated by fast cars, computers and watching endless football matches. If they don't appreciate these things in the same way as men, they will not enjoy conversations about them. If you spend an entire evening trying to extol the virtues of your latest computer motherboard upgrade, justifying the purchase of a Pentium against a mere 486 DX2 66, do not expect the date to be a success. Topics that most interest men are not guaranteed to interest women. An idea of what interests a woman will not only save her from boredom, but will actively engage her interest.

Society dictates the normal parameters of behaviour expected by the two genders, though obviously there are vast differences relating to age, religion and culture etc. As the world develops and progresses, ideas and values change accordingly. Since the turn of the century there have been vast changes in the traditional roles of men and women in society. The emergence of 'rock 'n' roll' in the 1950s was accompanied by a noticeable change in the freedom of young people. Over the last forty years many of the taboos that used to constrain the freedom of the youth have disappeared, allowing more flexible gender behaviour boundaries. But while this to some extent reduces the effect of conditioning, the inbuilt hormonal differences between men and women will always be present.

You might be asking what this has to do with approaching women? It demonstrates, above all, the complexity and difficulty men are faced with when they try to chat-up women. Although society might be blatantly open about relationships and sex, with every magazine telling you what women and men want from a relationship, there still remains the obstacle of forming the relationship. The media appears to be obsessed with articles on how to keep your woman, but little advice seems to be available on how to get the women in the first place. Are they assuming that it is a tricky area to deal with and is best left alone? It is tricky, but it needs to be tackled.

*Are you using the right frequency?*
To use an analogy, imagine that all chatting-up was done using radio transmitters and receivers. You set your dial for one frequency and start talking, but she's listening and talking on another frequency, so no communication is achieved. If you don't take the trouble to find out what her frequency is, you will make no progress. Although it may be impossible to find

instantly the precise frequency of someone you
don't know particularly well, it is possible to
know approximately which bands she is likely
to be using. These are general wavelengths that
apply to the majority of women. What all this
means is that there are groups of topics and
styles of conversation which are likely to interest
a woman, and it is important to remember these
when chatting-up. Those with a greater
understanding of the opposite sex will be able
to communicate with women on their own
frequency, the frequency which delivers the
greatest response.

If generalisations are to be made about women,
and before we come to the basics of chatting-up
it is important to understand them, it could be
said that they have a different set of values to
men. Men are usually portrayed as being the
tougher sex, showing a greater interest in areas
such as the achievement of power, money and
material goods. This is in sharp contrast to
women who tend to value love, communication
and friendship, though this is not to say that
there is not an element of all these in both men
and women. These differences occur due to
sexual conditioning rather than for biological
reasons. Women are just as capable of working
on cars and being DIY experts, and many of
them excel in these pursuits, but generally most
women are conditioned to the extent that they
find the idea of changing a set of spark plugs

about as exciting as the prospect of knitting a jumper would be to a man.

Men and women also have very conflicting ideas about relationships. Women generally are more concerned with relationships than men. They are not reluctant to talk about their personal feelings and regard it as an important part of a relationship. A man will normally only want to discuss his feelings if he is prompted by a woman or if something goes wrong. This is a recipe for disaster.

The objectives of this book are to offer some (hopefully) valuable advice on approaching women. This might be to aid in the delicate situation of asking a girl out on a date (and making the date a success), just to make friends with a girl or even to aid in the understanding of women in general. Feeling comfortable with women is not only important in the social context: to get on with women in the work environment is also useful. If you work for a woman, knowing how to approach her and get on with her can only be a positive move.

# Being single

That familiar tag, 'young free and single', describes a state of being to which even people in the happiest of relationships occasionally aspire. But it is one of those situations in which if you are not seeing anyone you believe life would be wonderful if you had someone with whom to share your life. So whatever situation you are in there will always be times when you wish you were in the other one. Unfortunately it is not always possible to pick and choose which situation you are in. If you are in a relationship then you are part of a couple and have to act accordingly.

Let's start by weighing up the advantages and disadvantages of being unattached. You might have not even considered the advantages, but when you start to think about them, life might not seem so bad!

If you're single you will be able to pursue all those admirable male pursuits without having to worry about what your girlfriend might think. If you yearn to stay in bed all day watching football, drinking lager and eating a mixture of cold curry and yesterday's pizza, there is no one stop you. However, if you were in a relationship you might just be settling down to watch the big match on a Saturday afternoon when your girlfriend tells you it's time to go shopping, and you have to go with her. You then spend the next couple of hours sitting outside the changing rooms of various clothes shops making polite comments about your girlfriend's figure.

Is this what you really want? Being in a relationship requires a certain amount of effort. Life will become a compromise to the needs of two, rather than just yourself. You have to be willing to make sacrifices. These sacrifices will cover things like the films you want to watch: she might want to see a horrible romantic comedy, you might want to see a nice violent thriller. When you are on your own you don't have these problems. The effort required is one of the main drawbacks to being in a relationship. When you are single and you've had a hard day, the prospect of a quiet evening at home doing absolutely nothing can be heavenly, but if you are attached your girlfriend might be expecting you to go out. This can leave you thinking, wouldn't it be nice to be single?

There are other advantages to being single: it is possible to channel all that spare time and energy into other pursuits that you would like to do but never had the time for. You might want to study in the evenings, restore an old car, or play golf every weekend. The number of hours available for such pursuits will be limited by a relationship. Much, though, depends on the type of relationship you have. Some couples are happy to spend all their time together whenever possible, others prefer to limit their time and get more out of each other seeing each other less frequently. The only problem is that there has to be agreement. If one partner wants to see the other every minute of the day and the other is content to make it once a week, there will be trouble.

Don't think that you should have a steady girlfriend just because some of your friends have them or because they say you should find yourself a woman. If you are single you may well experience the familiar situation where your best friends are always trying set you up with people they know. This can create those awful blind dates, two people who have been thrown together by friends wishing to play Cupid. You end up going on a date after much protest, probably because you would feel guilty about refusing their philanthropy. So there you are, two single people forced together. You begin to wonder why she is single, what could be wrong with her? You think she is probably thinking the same about you. Then you begin to think is she only there because her friends told her you are a sad and lonely male desperately seeking companionship. Forget these stupid thoughts, just enjoy yourself. She is probably as nervous as you are!

> ***If you possess the courage***
> ***to be single, you have the***
> ***courage to find a woman.***

The world we live in is heavily biased towards couples. Going to the cinema or eating out alone is viewed as odd. This stigma that surrounds a single person can stop that person from doing many of the things they really want to do. It could be said that being a determined bachelor takes as much courage as forming a relationship. If you possess the courage to be single, you have the courage to find a woman: it just needs to be channelled in a different way. This book will try to show you how to develop and channel that courage.

# Understanding women

For good communication a man has not only to become a good listener, he will also have to learn how to interpret a woman's expressions, feelings and moods. However, very few men truly understand women and probably very few women understand men. On this basis it is hardly surprising that so many relationships and, of course, marriages, end in disaster. At this stage you might not think it important to understand women when all you want is a date, but a basic understanding of women will help throughout the entire chatting-up process.

You might think that men and women speak the same language. Well, they don't. There are times when a women will say one thing and a man will interpret it in a completely different way. When a woman expresses her feelings she will often make use of exaggerated generalisations (men do too, but that's another story). When a woman says something like,

"You never want to go out,"

a man takes her literally and responds something like,

"But we went out last week."

What the woman really means is that she doesn't go out often enough, and wouldn't it be nice to go out tonight? Normally a man does not understand the true meaning of what a woman is saying. This breakdown in communication could be avoided if both parties explain exactly what they mean.

The communication aspect of any relationship is often under estimated: many marriages on the verge of breakdown could be saved if the partners can sit down at an early stage and talk about the problems they are experiencing. Often there are faults with both parties which can be resolved just by trying to understand what the problems are. It is unfortunate that it is often only the threat of divorce that makes people put in any effort. This is why although this book is fundamentally about forming a relationship this extra information can only be of benefit to a longer term relationship.

*Conflict*
Knowledge of the basic differences between men and women not only helps when chatting-up, but can also avoid conflict. Often, when couples argue, one of them will say,

"You just don't understand".

This is a common scenario. We usually expect the opposite sex to act and think in the same way as we do. Men often make the mistake of expecting women to behave in the same way as men, not only in the way they act but in other ways such as communicating and even sharing the same thoughts. It is not only men that are at fault, women usually forget to remember that men think differently to them.

If men and women gave more thought to these differences many arguments would be avoided. A frequent complaint of women (as well as 'you never want to talk') is,

"You never listen".

This may sound like a negligible crime but to women it is grounds for serious trouble. This information, apart from being essential for a successful relationship, should also be born in mind when on a date. One of the cardinal rules of dating is: if your date has just been telling you something important, perhaps about herself, don't immediately start talking about something that you are interested in. Give her some feedback on what she was saying or ask her to tell you more. If you ignore what she has to say, it will appear that you are only interested in talking about yourself and have no interest in what she has to say. This is hardly likely to create a good impression. (This topic is covered in greater detail in the chapter on Talking.)

# The basics of chatting-up

Many people find it hard to approach a member of the opposite sex. In fact, those who say they find it easy are probably either famous pop stars or liars. Approaching a woman for the first time is one of the hardest obstacles that has to be overcome in life, yet it has the potential to be one of the most rewarding.

People are surprised when they hear that an incredibly attractive person finds it hard to 'chat someone up'. If they find it hard, it is to say they lack confidence. Therefore good looks do not necessarily endow confidence in a man. It really has nothing to do with physical characteristics: to approach someone you need courage, if you lack this then you will find it hard make a move.

This fear can be due to a number of reasons. Shyness is the usual excuse, but there is normally more to it than that. A person may perceive themselves as being unattractive and feel that it is pointless even thinking about having a girlfriend. If you do have thoughts like this, you are going to have a lonely life. There are no reasons why anyone who wants a girlfriend cannot find one. The right image and approach can compensate for a lack of looks in nearly all cases, and remember that women suffer from all the same fears as men.

Another common hang-up is a difficulty in talking coherently to the opposite sex. You might find it easy talking to your friends but as soon as you have to talk to a woman the words cease to flow and you're left feeling self conscious and embarrassed.

These are the type of hurdles that can be overcome with a little thought and courage. Try writing down a list of your fears and think of ways of overcoming them. Don't be too ambitious: you can't expect to cure all your problems overnight. If you find it difficult talking or even being in the company of women, make an effort just to spend more time with women in any situation. This should build up your confidence and prepare you for the real thing.

So where do you start? There are no simple procedures that apply to all situations and types of women. Your 'act' must be tailored to each scenario. With enough experience, life will teach you all you need to know the hard way, but why make the mistakes for yourself when you can learn from others who have already made them? Every failed chat-up is a lesson in life, a demoralising kick in the teeth, and often a waste of money. For less than the price of a few drinks this book will enable you to bypass those failures and achieve success with women.

This book will be of use whatever your ultimate goal. It covers a wide range of topics from seeking a date or chatting-up someone in a bar to falling in love with an older woman or writing a love poem. It will tell you what to say, what not to say, when to give up, when to risk all and go for it. Use and interpret this book, however, according to your own talents, views and experience. We all have different tastes in women and it would be impossible to cover all eventualities. This book tries to cover most common situations and problems, and tries to show how most situations can be used to your advantage. The first part of the book covers different aspects of the chatting-up process, including your personal appearance and behaviour. These are the basic building blocks that can be used in the second part of the book in specific situations. These situations cover most of the common places in which chatting-up occurs: bars/pubs, nightclubs, the street, parties, the office, holidays, clubs, the library etc.

There are no 'tools of the trade' involved in chatting-up, but one thing is always useful to carry: name and address cards or business cards. They are easily available from machines these days, so there is no longer any excuse for clumsily looking for a pen and scribbling down your number on the back of a bus ticket. Just give her your card, and who knows - one day she may ring you?

Chatting-up is today easier to do than it has ever been. Society no longer imposes restrictions on courting couples. Women are free to date who they wish, to be in the company of a man 'un-chaperoned'. Young people are able to talk more freely about sex and relationships than were their parents. This means that chatting-up no longer requires the breaking through of inhibitions. We are playing on a level field with very few obstacles, man and woman, person to person. All you have to do is to make sure that your role as 'man' is played to the proper rules.

" NEVER bring this book with you on a date :"

This book will be useful whether you're a twelve

year old virgin about to go to a party, a retired widower, or any age in between. Just remember never to bring this book with you on a date. Learn the parts that are relevant to you, but act them out as if they have been learned by your own experience.

> *Chatting-up is today*
> *easier to do than*
> *it has ever been.*

# Psychology

This, in a sense, is what chatting-up is all about. There is a very fine line between a woman thinking your approach to her is cool and her thinking you're a jerk. What you say, how you say it, and your appearance are vital factors in swaying her opinion either way. If she finds you interesting, you're onto a winner. If you're boring, no chance. This does not mean to say that if you have led a fascinating life you should proceed with a lengthy monologue all about yourself. No matter how many famous people you went to school with, how fast your car is, or how large your bank balance may be, relating it all to a stranger in a nightclub will bore her to tears.

Paradoxically, people come away thinking someone is interesting if that person has asked questions about them, and has consistently shown interest in them. When chatting-up, never use the first person, always talk about the person you are chatting up. If she asks about you and your life, answer fully enough not to sound evasive, but don't use her question as a springboard to a verbal autobiography. Answer her question and then relate the topic back to her. She may well have asked the question out of politeness rather than out of genuine interest, and will welcome the opportunity to start talking once more about herself.

Another cardinal rule is never go on about an ex-girlfriend. Mentioning how attractive she was and all the wonderful times you had together will only antagonise your date. If you must mention her, it will suffice to say how long the relationship lasted and when it finished. Avoid referring to the ex-girlfriend in a totally negative way: your date may then start wondering whether you would refer to her in the same way if she went out with you for a while. It is far better to demonstrate your respect for women by mentioning a past girlfriend with brief fond respect, but without bitterness and without reproach.

*Freud*
Sigmund Freud did not have the benefit of a book like this when he went out on the pull. He had to develop his own theories, which include these:

**1.** *Everything we do springs from two motives: the sex urge and the desire to be great.*

The two can be seen as being intrinsically linked. A sexual encounter makes a man feel great, both in the sense of physical pleasure and in the sense of mental satisfaction, a feeling of success and a degree of power. Being successful at chatting-up women should enable you to feel great from both points of view.

2. *Popularity comes from being a good listener to other people, rather than talking about yourself.*

The term popularity does not necessarily mean you need to be popular with lots of women at once: one will do. Being a good listener to one woman will make you 'popular' with her. If you never listen to her and just talk about yourself, she will consider you a bore.

An important rule of dating is never to let a woman know how desperate you are. Drooling all over a woman will probably make her sick and run a mile. It is all a matter of balance: keep the scales level and you stand a better chance. If a woman comes on strong, don't instantly fall at her feet, show a certain degree of self control. However, do not be too cold or you will lose her completely.

Trying to give comprehensive advice on how to act with women is an almost impossible task. No one woman has the same ideas and values. One inexplicable feature of women is that they do not always prefer a man who is kind, trustworthy and loving. Many women seem to enjoy going out with men who treat them badly, even if they won't openly admit it. This utterly bewilders men who try to treat women with respect. The explanation for this strange behaviour has been attributed to the fact that women like the excitement and the challenge of taming a wild man. Sometimes it can seem as if you are in a *Catch 22* situation: if you're nice to her she may find you boring, but if you try to act mean it could backfire and she'll dump you. Just beware!

# Positive thinking and self confidence

Self confidence is the foundation upon which you will build your entire technique. Without self confidence your technique will be hollow. Don't miss any opportunity: this is a golden rule of being successful. There are thousands of opportunities that are missed due to inhibitions and lack of preparation. If you only make an attempt to chat-up a girl when in the pub, you are missing out on the other potentially fruitful situations.

> *Self confidence*
> *is the foundation*
> *upon which you will build*
> *your entire technique.*

You might be surprised at the success you can achieve if you develop the attitude - 'what have I got to lose?' OK, so if it is someone you work with and she turns you down, it might cause a slight embarrassment, but after a few days it will all be forgotten. This book is not so much trying to encourage you go from one woman to the next, more it is trying to help you get the woman you want (or the women in some cases). Women admit that if they know that a person is interested in them, they are more likely to fancy that person. If the woman has no idea that you are interested, it is less likely that anything will ever happen.

Always be ready. Always look your 'best' even if you don't expect to meet a girl. You might meet the girl of your dreams one morning as you make the daily trip in an overcoat and slippers to get the papers from the local shop across the road. You look terrible, she looks great: opportunity wasted.

Occasionally the situation might arise where you are on a train or a tube and you get chatting to the girl next to you. She is attractive, funny, and intelligent. You sense that there is a spark between you, then she says this is her stop. There is a lingering silence, and neither has the courage to say anything but goodbye. You would both like to ask for the other's phone number, but you cannot do so. She leaves, and you are left feeling that you have wasted a chance to change your life for the better. This is the sort of scenario that occurs frequently.

The way to avoid this unfortunate situation is to carry address cards and give one to any girl you meet in this manner. You could say something like,

"I don't normally do this sort of thing, but here's my number - perhaps we could meet for lunch some time? Give me a call if you'd like that."

Another aspect of positive thinking is coping with the way you look and not letting it be a problem. The vast majority of men would probably like to change their appearance in some way if they could. They all see themselves as in some way ugly, and this hinders their confidence when dealing with the opposite sex.

The first point to remember is that whether or not most people think they are ugly, most people eventually find love in the end, no matter how disfigured they may be. You may see a repulsive man with a beautiful woman on his arm, and wonder how he did it? This is a common occurrence, and is often answered by money. But it could be that he has an endearing personality, that the woman fell in love with his character rather than his body. Certainly, this is what counts in a long term relationship. But getting started with character alone is much more difficult unless you know the woman in the first place.

Even if cultivating an attractive personality is easy, getting a woman close enough to be able to appreciate it is much harder. Instead (or preferably as well), why not spend a few years preparing for the financial approach? A number of years of determined hard work, a little imagination and a little luck, could change your standard of living immeasurably. The most common ways of doing this are through simply working extra hard at your existing job in order to be noticed by management and achieve promotion, attending evening classes to earn qualifications that will smooth the path to promotion or a better job, or by running your own small business.

These methods will not pay dividends overnight, but if marriage is your ultimate goal then remember that it is a long term commitment, and to achieve it through having more money requires a medium term investment in your time and energy. Money will not necessarily generate sincerity in a woman, but it is a great aphrodisiac.

If you want to have the advantages of being 'rich' without really having very much money, it is possible to develop an image of wealth and prosperity on an average income. Good taste is the prerequisite here: a smart, slightly eccentric classic car, smart clothes and a refined manner. Save the beer money for opera tickets, read the 'quality' newspapers, and don't go on package holidays. (People with class don't go on holiday. They 'travel'.)

Sometimes your confidence is affected by one physical feature with which you are dissatisfied. Why not do something about it? Why not investigate the possibility of cosmetic surgery? There are many physical features that can be changed with simple cosmetic operations. This includes hair, teeth, skin, facial features and other parts of the body. Clinics can give advice as to individual needs, and offer a discreet professional service.

Another approach to improving your confidence is to concentrate on your body rather than on your face. A good body, a cool image and self-confidence (with an ugly face) are more appealing than a good looking but dull and boring person. Join a local gym so that you can work-out, if not for body-building then at least to shed some lard from your stomach.

What can you do if you are so good looking that girls are afraid to approach you? This is a rare problem, but it makes it difficult to chat-up ordinary, 'nice' girls. Try to reverse some of the advice on hair and clothes, to make yourself more approachable.

# Image

## External image

A person's image is made up of a number of attributes. There are some features that are fixed, but generally an image is created by a person and will reflect the personality of that person. These features include clothes, hairstyle, language, attitude etc. Because an image normally mirrors the personality, there is no point in trying to be someone you are not. There are, however, subtle changes that can be made. It is important to think hard about the image you portray at the moment. It very easy to be complacent and to overlook any faults. If you find it hard to be objective perhaps ask a friend to give you a few ideas.

In changing your image to one that will be more appealing to women, try first to weed out all the negative attributes and build your new image on a 'clean slate'. Ask yourself: do I make an effort to be friendly to women? Do I show off when I talk to women (women usually hate men who wallow in their own glory)? There are even more basic questions that you should ask yourself: do I have bad breath or unsightly personal habits?

## Here are a few instant turn-offs:

Unpleasant body odour
Greasy hair
'Dull' hair
Dirty clothes
Unfashionable clothes
Picking one's nose
Scratching one's extremities

It is important, as mentioned earlier, to have an image that fits your personality. If you are naturally a quiet person, then dressing in flamboyant clothes will not really suit you. But try to make an effort to change your image to some extent, eliminating all negative aspects at the very least. Take notice of what people your age seem to be wearing when they are talking to girls in the pub. Look at their hairstyles: are they long, short or weird? Do they have sideburns, beards or moustaches? Look at their shoes. Then look at your own shoes. Could you change your image to be able to blend in with these people? Would you feel strange looking like that? At first, everyone feels strange with a new image, but with enough courage to live with that image for a few days it will soon become second nature.

Successful chatting-up is dependent upon image

to an extent that is perhaps unfair. To hide your personality behind an image that is not really 'you' seems false. People dress themselves to appear to be something they are not, but only in order to become 'acceptable', to be accepted by a member of the opposite sex. Once someone gets to know you, your true personality will be more important than your chosen image. The image is just a stepping stone to your real character, but without that stepping stone few women will get the chance to discover your personality.

There is a certain amount of commercialism involved in 'chatting-up': it involves selling yourself. This does not mean you stand in the pub with a 'for sale' sign on your back, though perhaps it might work? Selling yourself literally means making yourself attractive to the prospective client. In a chat-up situation, the first thirty seconds of contact are all you have to grab her attention and win her over. It's similar to a TV advert: you are the product and the woman is the market. If the advert is poor or makes you cringe you are unlikely to be interested in that product. What are your best selling points? List them, then read them objectively, as a woman. Would she be interested? If not, think about why. Could you market yourself better?

*Cars*
The British nation appears to be obsessed with

cars. The car you drive makes as much as a statement about yourself as the clothes you wear. Unfortunately a person is often judged on these superficial characteristics: you might argue that these material things are not important and you only want a women if she will accept you for who you are. Well, that's fair enough, but you might have to wait a while.

So what car should you be driving? Obviously there are constraints such as money and other practicalities, but here are some ideas.

If you're after the sort of woman who will be impressed by an Escort that says XR3i in huge letters on the rear screen, then get yourself one. If you have a modicum of taste, try something more subtle like a Saab (not the saloon), a VW Golf or a Renault 5. Any classic car will do: Beetles and Morris Minors are the staple diet here, embellished by Spitfires, MGs, VW Campers. Never, ever, ever buy a Metro.

The main thing with cars is not to drive something that a woman will be embarrassed to be seen in. Large sums of money do not need to be spent in order to achieve this; just common sense in avoiding 'boring' cars or cars that are associated with middle age and a lack of imagination or character (such as metallic brown Japanese saloons).

*Phones*

What about mobile phones? As the prices of these vital personal accessories are tumbling you might ask yourself the question should I buy one or not? Many people believe they are still a bit naff, yet sales are booming.

If you give a girl your mobile telephone number, the chances are she will be impressed. She may not show it, indeed she may vomit copiously at the sight of it, but deep down she will know that you are going places. Phones are becoming cheaper all the time, with low use tariffs offering a lower monthly rental charge to those who only want them for posing.

# Self image

More important than your external image, however, is your self image. You must value yourself, have a sense of worth. Be aware of your value, both in moral terms and practical terms. If you have ever excelled in anything, try to bring that to mind before you begin chatting-up. This is not in order to tell her all about it, but to boost your self-confidence generally. If you have successfully chatted someone up before but are nervous about doing it with someone else, remember the first time and convince yourself that you can do it again.

Your external image is important in making the first impression, but if you are a nervous wreck beneath it, or if you do not feel worthy of it, she will sense this and may lose interest. At the same time, if you develop a cool image externally, this may reap dividends with your self-confidence. Everyone is different, but try to make the most of your image and confidence. One without the other will make chatting-up that much harder.

*Fashion*
Fashions come and go year by year, month by month and even week by week. Whatever was in vogue once is unlikely to be in fashion any longer. This not only applies to clothes, but to music, cars, food and even lager.

So what has this got to do with chatting-up women? Well, if you wear a duffel coat and trousers that don't reach your ankles and wonder why people who follow the latest silly fashions get off with more girls than you, it might be wise to think about the shallowness and fickleness of some girls. They may, in your opinion, be foolish to fall for men whose only interests are pop music and clothes, whereas you may be knowledgeable about modern railway systems and insects, but if you want them to take any notice of you it will be necessary to change your style. Swallow your pride and your principles, try to look like everyone else, and acceptance by the female fraternity should soon follow. Lack of fashion sense can usually be compensated for by an appealing charisma and charming eccentricity, but this normally comes with age and should not be relied upon in youth.

In some cases retro chic can provide an attraction. The ghastly fashions of the Seventies were mocked with the hindsight of a few years, but were finally rekindled, though only to a small extent, among those at the very heart of the fashion scene. There is a subtle difference between this and bad taste, so be very careful. It is safer to avoid fringe trends such as these and stick to mainstream 'blokes in the pub' styles.

*Clothes*
"The apparel oft proclaims the man," as Polonius put it with characteristic pomposity. White socks and a suit tell more about you than a thousand words. Yet some people still wear them in the belief that they are smart. The red braces and stripey shirt favoured by city types in the late eighties have also gone. Enter the nineties man. Forget the grunge image, Dr. Martens, ripped T-shirts and matted hair, go for the smart but casual look.

This does not require vast expenditure on clothes. Don't buy cheap quality garments, just try to do most of your clothes shopping during the sales. Smart, tasteful clothes do not necessarily cost more than scruffy or tasteless clothes. Don't think that a girl will be impressed with you if you spend a fortune on a vile Italian designer shirt and then you say you can't afford to buy her a drink.

The tight trouser syndrome is also out. You might be hung like a donkey but subtlety is preferred. Your trousers should always reach your shoes, not like a pair of pedal pushers.

Attention to detail is important. A cheap digital watch on your wrist can ruin an entire image (avoid digital watches at all costs). Jeans can be worn, but never with training shoes. Leave such combinations for children. In the adult world, real shoes must be worn. Girls tend to be more observant than men so remember to do up your flies; there is nothing quite as embarrassing as talking to a girl, then realising that your flies were undone and your shirt was poking out. Or worse.

Girls will also notice if your attire mixes patterns with stripes or if your hair colour clashes with the clothes. These may not be important on a global scale, but it is nevertheless best not to advertise the fact that you have no taste. If you want to play safe with colours and patterns, it is hard to go wrong with a kind of beatnik 'black all over' image, provided you don't end up looking like an SAS soldier.

The Medallion Man, if you think that women find it attractive to see your shirt undone to the navel, with enough gold chains to supply the Royal Mint for a week, combined with a nylon chest wig, think again.

*Hair*
Long hair can cover up facial inadequacies, and so long as it's still in fashion and you don't need to be taken seriously at work or elsewhere it is a good idea to let it grow. As a statement, long hair says 'I'm unable to be original in my looks, so I'm copying everyone else who appears to be mildly trendy and I don't care if loads of blokes fancy me from behind', but don't let that put you off. If you play guitar then you've probably got long hair anyway, so it doesn't matter.

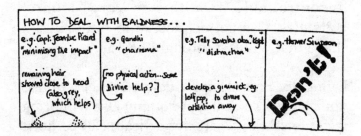

HOW TO DEAL WITH BALDNESS...

| e.g. Capt. Jean-Luc Picard "minimising the impact" | e.g. Gandhi "charisma" | e.g. Tely Savalas aka "Kojak" "distraction" | e.g. Homer Simpson |
|---|---|---|---|
| remaining hair shaved close to head (also grey, which helps) | [no physical action...some Divine help?] | develop a gimmick, e.g. lollipop, to draw attention away | Don't! |

There is no point in printing a guide that tells you exactly how to have your hair cut. The only thing to do is to look closely at other people and try to get a haircut similar to theirs. Once you do this, make sure you check the current fashions regularly. Otherwise you may end up like the thousands of middle-aged men who today still wear their teddy-boy's haircut from the Fifties, or the famous aging hippies whose fashion clocks stopped in 1972. Every six to twelve months is a good time to review your hairstyle if you have made it particularly fashionable. Otherwise, play safe with a short, neat 'businesslike' haircut that requires little attention and is less likely to go out of fashion quickly.

There is a bewildering range of hair care products available suitable for all hair types: shampoos, conditioners, gels etc. If you have greasy hair wash it regularly and if you have uncontrollable or thin hair try using a hair gel to hold it in place. The trouble with clean, washed hair is that it often goes limp and uncontrollable, resulting in very 'square' hairstyles. Use gel or mousse to put it into a shape that will last through the day.

Dying your hair is not usually necessary unless your mop is so dull that nothing else will bring it to life. 'Sun-ins' are very cheap, can be done at home from the packet, and will lighten the hair colour gently. But for greatest impact why not go for total blond or jet black? If you have not done this before it would be better to leave it to the capable hands of your hairdresser.

The most vital thing to recognise if you are having trouble chatting-up women is whether you have 'square' hair. If it is combed with an immaculate side parting that shows a clear line of scalp from your ear to the back of you head, or if it is brushed straight down to your eyebrows in the same way you have done it since you were a child, it might be time for a change. You may not want to make your hair 'trendy', but if the girls perceive it as being square, they will think of you as square, and hence boring. They won't give you a chance. Get yourself a more outrageous haircut and give yourself a chance.

If you are lacking in hair, there are two basic rules. The first is: do not grow it long on one side and try to glue it in strands across your forehead. This NEVER works successfully. The second is: be wary of wigs. Often they look obvious, and even if she doesn't notice it until you get into bed, she may feel conned, embarrassed, or disgusted when it comes off during passionate lovemaking. Even if it survives this, she will find out eventually if it turns into a serious relationship.

A hat is perfectly acceptable, provided it looks good in the context of the environment in which you find yourself. If you are at the races at Ascot, for instance, you will not stand out from the crowd as someone who is blatantly wearing a hat to cover their follicular deficiency. But you might raise suspicions if you are in a swimming pool.

An effective way to minimise the impact of a bald patch is to shave your hair very short, so that any thin parts do not stand out. This technique can be effective if you grow your stubble to the same length.

*Facial Hair*
If you want to have a moustache or a beard, make sure you are capable of growing one before launching some wispy hairs upon the world. Sideburns, bits of beards and designer stubble move in and out of fashion frequently. Whatever you have, so long as it's not blatantly out of fashion, you are marginally more likely to succeed. Even if you look a complete pratt, so long as some pop star in *Melody Maker* looks similarly afflicted that week, you should be OK.

*Smells*
Use a good de-odourant every morning: roll-ons are very reliable. Bathe or shower before a date if possible. It should not be necessary to spend money on expensive aftershave, unless it significantly increases your self confidence, but use sparingly if at all. Water makes a good

aftershave and comes out of a tap. Splashing macho odours all over can be just as bad as natural odour if it makes it too clear that you're desperate to score, but modest use of pleasant smelling aftershave may help.

Watch your breath. Anyone can develop bad breath without realising, and it can be a real turn-off. Usually breath will start to smell after each meal. Brush your teeth before a date, even if you expect to be eating before you kiss, and have some mints in your pocket as a stand-by.

It is now possible to buy 'female attracting' scents in spray form, usually pheromone. These are the smells that encourage mating among animals, and may well appeal to a girl's subconscious and help to make her attracted to you. In the right environment they can work wonders. Even if this doesn't occur, they may well serve as a valuable psychological crutch. If you think that the spray is working, you will act with greater confidence and hence will have greater appeal.

# Alcohol

Most of us are only too aware of the possible effects of alcohol. Whether your favourite tipple is lager, bitter, wine or whisky, the end result of a few glasses is the same. It can give you that little bit of Dutch courage that you need in order to approach a woman. Booze is most effective in a rowdy party situation where you drink by the bottle rather than by the glass, and you can sneak outside or upstairs with her. At a bar you have to fork out money constantly and in a public library it's difficult to keep silent.

It is vital to make the most of a girl's inebriation before the effects wear off. When she's drunk, something ridiculous like the following can work very well,

"Would you like to come and see my stamp collection - it's outside in that shadowy area over there?"

There is less of a need for subtlety when the sharp corners of your amateurish chat-up lines are blurred by an alcoholic haze. Jokes are funnier, embarrassment is diminished, and the corniest and most blatant chat-up lines suddenly transform into aphorisms worthy of Oscar Wilde.

Getting drunk yourself is also a great idea in the right situation, provided it makes you confident and not violently sick. Ask a friend which category you come under if you can't remember. Don't drink so much that you fall over, as this won't impress anyone.

One of the biggest psychological blocks in chatting-up is the initial approach. Get through that first couple of minutes and things will get a lot easier. A moderate amount of alcohol in your blood can make that first approach very much easier. You will be less afraid of the consequences of rejection, and will come across as more confident and less farty (provided you can still form a coherent sentence). However, this approach can backfire if you appear to be drunk and insincere. If she is desperate, she will know that she can take advantage of this. If she is also drunk she won't notice. But if she is sober, she will think you are pathetic and boring if you are blatantly drunk.

Drinks to avoid: anything with an umbrella or cherries in it. If you want to maintain a macho image, stick to pints. In some rougher areas, those who only want to drink half a pint order it in a pint glass to avoid being beaten up. Otherwise, drink whatever you prefer, bearing in mind the suitability of the drink to the establishment: beer is fine for pubs, but wine is usually more appropriate for restaurants.

# Telephoning

Apart from the personal approach, the next most popular method of asking someone out is by using the telephone. If you find it hard to approach someone in the flesh, using the telephone may be your best bet. You may have been given a phone number of a girl you have met, or may just have looked in the phone book for the number of a girl that you know and decide to ask her out.

Picking up the phone can be just as daunting as asking someone out face to face, but remember you have nothing to lose. Let us suppose you have met a girl and exchanged numbers. It may have been on a train, at the pub, or by mutual introduction. Wherever it was, your conversation will have been brief, and your knowledge of her character will be skimpy. When to phone after exchanging numbers? Should you phone first, or play it cool and wait for her to call you? This is a dangerous psychological game, since you might end up waiting forever. If you phone too soon, you'll appear too keen, which puts her in a dominant position and might put her off. Two or three days is usually sufficient time for your follow up to appear cool and laid-back. Don't wait any longer than that for her to phone. If you want to give the relationship a chance, make the move yourself. Obviously, it puts you in a stronger position if she does phone first, but don't worry if she doesn't.

If her response is clearly negative when you phone, don't keep pestering her on the phone each day until she agrees to meet you. Although in the old films the lover who keeps on trying despite constant rejection, declaring his love for her with flowers, gifts and phone calls, finally gets to marry her, in reality you will end up with a court injunction banning you from any contact with her. Learn when to give up.

If she sounds remotely pleased to hear from you, assuming she remembers who you are, keep the tone as casual and unimportant as you can.

Don't make it sound as if your entire future happiness depends on her response. Make it clear that you think meeting her again would be a great idea, but that it doesn't matter if she can't make it since you've got one or two other things to do. If a date with just the two of you might sound too oppressive for her, suggest she come with a group of friends, preferably mutual ones.

The conversation may be a little stilted if you or she is shy, so don't stretch the conversation beyond a time that you can comfortably manage. When people first get to know each other, there may little in common to talk about. If a long, embarrassed pause occurs, wind up to the conversation quickly, going straight for the question,

"Would you like to come for a drink later this week?"

or whatever the purpose of the call is. Make sure there is a purpose, by the way. Note that saying later this week is less specific than naming a particular day, and reduces her opportunity for saying no. It is always useful to avoid backing yourself into a corner by being too specific about a place (she may not like it) or a time (she may be busy) when first asking someone out.

*Other reasons (excuses) for calling could include:*

i) you are really bored and would like to do something with her;

ii) to ask her to a party (if this party is fictional, why not ring again the night before and explain that it has been cancelled, so why don't the two of you do something together?);

iii) you bumped into a mutual friend today, which reminded you of her;

iv) you have a question for her that you know comes within her area of specialist knowledge or interest;

v) did she leave something behind when you last met? (You know she didn't, but that doesn't matter.)

Provided she sounds willing to continue chatting on the phone, talk about her and ask about her interests in the same way that you would in a face to face situation. Find out things about her that could influence the way you dress or act on the subsequent date, eg. is she vegetarian? Listen and respond to what she says. This may sound obvious, but often people do not listen, merely waiting for a break in the other person's speech in order to say what they had already decided to say. There is no need to suppress your opinions completely, but do not smother hers with yours.

One of life's worst nightmares is plucking up the courage to ring her, only for the phone to be answered by a male voice. Try not to let your shock and disappointment show. Ask to speak to her in a relaxed manner, rather than the guilty manner which will instinctively come to the fore. Your heart will be telling you that this is her boyfriend or husband, who will be suspicious of you, but your head will be trying to point out that he is more likely to be a flatmate, relative, or just a friend. Act cool, ask her who it was that answered the phone. If you want to sound really disinterested, tell her that her boyfriend sounds like a nice bloke. If she thanks you and agrees, you've got problems. If she says that you spoke to Hilda who has a rather deep voice, all will be well.

# Where to go on a date

This decision will have to be given some thought. Of course you might be going out with a group of friends which makes the situation a little easier. If it is just two of you, you will have to make the following decision: do you want a date where you can talk and get to know each other, or perhaps go to see a film where conversation is limited? If conversation is your weak point, opt for the film. That way you will talk for only a few minutes afterwards, and at least you will have something to talk about (ie the film).

With most girls, avoid going to Halfords or a scrap metal yard for the first date. Try to go somewhere that they find interesting or exciting. She may be more impressed if you offer her dinner rather than a drink, but you are also making a bigger commitment. Don't waste too much money at this early stage unless you really can afford it. You can never be sure of success, and indeed will never necessarily earn it, no matter how much money is spent.

If you are going to a pub, avoid one where she is likely to meet most of her friends. She will either be ill at ease with you, or will completely ignore you. To get to know her, choose a quiet pub.

The cinema is a traditional dating ground, but is not the place for chatting-up. Few cinemas have double seats in the back row with plenty of leg-over room these days, and cuddling over an arm rest can be uncomfortable.

Asking her to a party or a ball is usually a good bet. Either will give you plenty of opportunities for chatting her up, and she is more likely to accept even if she is unsure about you, since she will not be committed to talking just to you all evening.

If you have a local theatre, why not try the approach,

"Someone has given me a couple of tickets for the play - do you want to come?"

If she accepts, rush out and buy a couple of tickets. The same goes for a concert.

Going for a walk is a great way to get to know someone, with no distractions. If you live close to pleasant countryside or a beach, take her for a walk with a picnic, or buy her lunch at a pub.

# Handling the date

A first date with someone is just as nerve-racking as an exam, a driving test, or a visit to the dentist. Men can worry, they can panic, and they arrive at the date like quivering lumps of jelly, incoherent and clumsy, not being 'themselves' and not even managing to put up the 'cool' image they have been trying for weeks to cultivate. Is this you? Hopefully not, but if it is then there are a few simple techniques that can help to calm those nerves before she arrives.

First of all, allow enough time to prepare for the date so that you are not rushed and flushed. If you arrive sweaty and angry after a hurried journey she will immediately see you in a negative and less attractive mood, so make sure you need no more than a leisurely drive or stroll to get there. On the other hand, don't prepare yourself in the afternoon for a rendezvous at eight in the evening. If you are left with three of four hours with nothing to do, it will be a bad, nail-biting experience. You will spend those hours worrying about the date, about whether your hair will go out of place before you get there, whether your aftershave will have worn off and your breath will have begun to smell. Avoid this by planning the preparation for the date like a military operation, allowing no more than five or ten minutes extra. As long as you have something to do in the hours before the date, there will be less opportunity for worrying.

During those inevitable reflective moments before the date, be realistic about what you expect to happen. Don't be pessimistic from the start, convincing yourself that she will hate you at first sight: this may lessen the surprise of possible subsequent failure or rejection, but it will also make that failure more likely. Success is more easily achieved with a positive, but not overconfident, mood. Overconfidence begets mistakes, a positive mood gives you every advantage possible. Think to yourself that you will be charming, she will like you, and you will show her the best sides of your personality.

---

**Set a modest target
for a first date:
rather than sex this should be
to become a friend of hers.**

---

Set a modest target for a first date: rather than sex this should be to become a friend of hers, someone with whom she feels comfortable and someone she can trust. If all goes well, aim for a 'goodnight kiss' after the second date, and so on. It will never guarantee success (nothing does!) but it will maximise your chances. Obviously, situations arise in which relationships can develop much faster than this, but aiming to be just a friend rather than a lover on the first date is often a good way to develop a longer lasting relationship. By not forcing your attentions on her on the first date you are likely to earn her respect as a man of restraint and self control. You will not seem desperate or inexperienced, just calm and mature.

To deal with pre-date nerves, either make sure you have enough things to do before the date to keep your mind occupied, or take deep breaths for a few minutes in order to relax the mind and the body. Remember that your date will probably be just as nervous as you are, and think about how funny this situation would be to an objective onlooker: two people terrified of meeting each other, worried that the other person won't like them, yet very keen to meet.

When you do meet for the first time, how do you greet her? In some circles a kiss on the cheek would be normal, but in others it might seem too overtly sexual. You could shake hands, and maybe kiss her on the cheek while you are shaking hands, but again to do both can seem over-familiar. The safest method, least likely to offend or to put her under pressure, is to shake hands warmly but not lingeringly. Smile broadly and look her in the eye, rather than grinning weakly and looking at the ground. Say something like,

"Hi, you must be . . .? Did you find this place alright?"

Asking about her journey is a very easy way of breaking the conversational ice. It is not an intimate personal question, it avoids the embarrassing fact that you are on a date, and it can be answered without thinking. You and she will still be nervous at this stage, so questions and answers that require little coherent thought will start things off more smoothly. Assuming you are meeting in a bar of some sort, now ask her something like,

"So what would you like to drink?"

If you go to get the drinks, you both have a few moments alone to compose yourselves, to let your first impressions of each other sink in, and to decide how you are going to tackle the evening. When you come back, the ice can be broken still further by saying something like,

"This is very embarrassing, isn't it? It seems very artificial. Why don't you just tell me about your day?"

A speech like that shows that you are not overconfident, but you are not so shy that you can't admit embarrassment. You are also taking control of the conversation without being bossy or cocky. Laughing off the awkwardness of the situation and then asking her to tell you something as straightforward as what her day was like puts her more at ease, and gets her talking. Stick to trivialities for the first few minutes until you get used to talking to her, then ask about her job or studies, her home, her family, her last holiday, her next holiday, what she normally does at weekends etc. While it is best to let her talk about herself more than you do about yourself, try not to make it seem like an interview. Give plenty of feedback, but don't get stuck talking about yourself when it is not relevant to what she has said.

When it comes to the end of the date, remember your original objective. Do you want her to respect you and give you a chance to form a long term relationship? It is not always true that relationships that start quickly end quickly, and vice versa, but taking things slowly at the start at least indicates that you are serious about her, not just after a 'one night stand'.

If you are after a one night stand, the way you say goodbye should indicate that you don't really want to leave her at all. Be bold in going for the goodbye kiss that will show her that you would rather spend more time with her. If this is made clear to her, she then has the choice of pushing you away and saying a firm goodbye, or of saying that the night is young and asking where you want to go now.

If you want to take things slowly and respectfully, it is nevertheless polite to give her the opportunity for a passionate kiss if that is what she wants. Say goodbye somewhere private, not in the centre of a restaurant or bar. If possible, accompany her to her house, but don't invite yourself in. Kiss her on the cheek, touch her on the arm, and tell her you had a wonderful evening. This is unthreatening behaviour that shows affection without being too sexual. If she wants to respond with a full embrace, then she will. Otherwise, leave it for a later date with her.

If you are invited into her house, don't assume you will be spending the night there. It is more likely than not that things will get a little physical, but, unless she makes it absolutely clear that she wants you to stay, offer to leave after an hour or so. This will prompt her either to say that you can stay if you want, or to fetch your coat for you. An invitation to come into her house for a drink is not an invitation for sex, so again be realistic as to what you expect. Remember that pushing her too far on the first date will lessen the chances of there ever being a second date with her. But holding back and not initiating sexual advances on the first date will make any such advances on a second date that much more likely to succeed.

# Impressing

Chatting-up is about impressing a girl in the sense of making a good first impression. Some men take it upon themselves to continue trying to impress throughout the date, in a self conscious attempt to prove their masculinity. This is not as important these days as it was in the days of our simian ancestors, since humans can now make use of lively wit and intelligence rather than swinging from the highest branches with their tackle showing. This has not stopped some men, though, from driving up the High Street at full speed past a group of unimpressed girls, or from drinking lager until their bladders explode. Known as macho play, this is no longer a biological necessity, but the instinct still persists in some.

It is possible to impress a girl with your body, but having a good, fit body is not an easy option. It requires self-regulation with regard to diet and exercise, but if you can maintain good habits in these respects you should find it most worthwhile.

Do you have any performing talent? Being a performer is a sure way of improving your sex appeal. Even the ugliest rock stars have queues of women waiting to sleep with them when they get off stage. You don't need to be a star, but if you perform in amateur dramatics, sing at a college gig or even busk in a dark subway, your chances of successfully chatting-up any member of the audience are significantly increased. For a start, you have something in common - you performed, she watched. You are also interesting to her - why did you perform that song? How did you get the gig? Were you nervous? Be careful not to talk in detail about your TV appearances etc, though. Name-dropping really is very dull for the other person. Be discreet and modest, and turn the conversation to her as soon as she has asked you what she really wants to know about your performance, which won't be much.

# Talking

Whatever the context in which you find yourself chatting someone up, what you say is vital to the way in which she perceives you. Those few sentences are her main clue to your personality (together with your clothes and hair etc.), so your topics and phrases are vital. Having said that, don't be so worried about saying the right thing that you end up completely tongue-tied. Sometimes being shy can work to your advantage: a girl will know that you are not just another smooth tongued Casanova who is using his charm on yet another girl. If you can talk in a natural and relaxed manner, then fine. If not, read on.

The main thing to remember is don't talk about yourself. This cannot be over-emphasised. It is a vital component in making a good impression when chatting-up. Talk about her hair, her clothes, her job/studies, home town/country, car (not in too much detail though - something along the lines of "I see you drive a red car. That's a nice colour." will be enough not to alienate her). Ask what she likes to drink, what countries she has visited, what her husband does for a living. Resist the temptation, whenever she replies to one of your questions, to turn the conversation to yourself,

"What are you studying," you ask her.

"Biology," she replies.

"I study Maths. It's great. Do you know what a hypotenuse is?" etc.

Far better to follow up her reply with questions about the course, what she finds interesting about it, where it's leading her. This will get her talking about the things that interest her, rather than what interests you. She'll find out about your mathematical prowess in due course; let her have her way this time.

Refer to the A-Z of chat-up lines for a varied arsenal of opening gambits, but remember that we cannot provide a full script for you to stick to. The best and probably most successful line is simply,

"Can I buy you a drink?"

after which you can go on to ask if she always drinks that, what her name is, etc. Other lines are equally valid in different situations, and some can be used to follow up the others. Often it is a good idea to ask a question that requires a more elaborate answer than yes or no. For example,

"Do you come here often?"

can only be replied with,

"Yes," or "No".

This will start the conversation off in a stilted way, and does not automatically lead anywhere. A better line would be,

"I'm sure I've seen you here before. My name's . . . What do you think of this place?"

This gives her the opportunity to say much more in return. Even if she has never been there before, she will feel obliged to introduce herself, and from then on you can ask her any other questions.

There are a few topics that are best avoided when chatting-up, though they are fairly obvious. These include: football, computers, cars, lager, fighting, DIY, trains, your wife, your diseases. Far better to concentrate on her job, her house, her interests current affairs, her taste in food, clothes and men. Compliment her on her taste, particularly on her clothes or her hair.

If she tells you about her problems, don't tell her they are unimportant because they can easily be solved in a logical manner. Odd though it may seem, she will appreciate sympathy more than practicality. Just give her your full attention and listen carefully, giving occasional responsive noises such as 'uhmm' or 'yes'.

*Bullshit*
Since chatting-up is all about making an initial impression and creating an image of yourself, it can be a severe disadvantage if you are a nobody who has led an extremely dull life. If you are after a quick fling, it can be worth embellishing your curriculum vitae with whatever you think will make a girl regard you as more interesting or a 'better pull'. For one night stands, when you're away from home or on holiday and don't expect or want to see the girl again, you can adopt an entirely false persona for the evening - doctor, city broker, roadsweeper (for inversely snobbish Oxbridge women). Enjoy yourself.

Obviously this tactic only works until she finds out about it, so don't play this card if you want her to trust and respect you in the long term.

Keep the bullshit realistic. If your accent is more Ilford than Oxford then don't pretend to be a minor aristocrat. Don't say you're a doctor if you don't know where her sternum is. Basically, don't get out of your depth, unless you are such a boring person that it's your only chance. If you are going to tell a lie to impress, try to make sure you can't be caught out. If caught out, laugh it off as a practical joke.

When on home ground or when you want the relationship to develop, play safe and keep the lies small and white. Give your job a more exciting description:

"I work in the communications business,"

instead of,

"I'm a postman."

Say you own two cars, but the BMW is being serviced this week, so you're relying on the Mini for the moment.

Bullshit also applies to your attitude towards her. She may be an opera buff, she may have a fetish for Norwegian fjords and spend most of the evening reminiscing about them. Unless you are cool enough to walk away from such a bore, in which case you probably have enough confidence and experience not to need this book, you should put up with her monologue. Indeed, you should actively encourage her, asking intelligent questions about her specialist subject and pretending you have a genuine interest and maybe a little knowledge of it. Yes, you went to several operas last year (too many to name), yes you went to the fjords one summer and thought they were the most beautiful place on earth. She will love you for it.

Cyrano de Bergerac fed his handsome, but rather brain-dead, chum with poetry and beautiful words in order to help him woo his girl, and she fell for it instantly, until she realised they were not his own thoughts. Practise the art of bullshitting with the bullshit game - take it in turns to talk for thirty seconds convincingly on a subject nominated by a friend about which you know nothing. Beware of running out of borrowed poetry like Cyrano's chum. Far better if you can cultivate original poetry and beauty yourself as and when it is needed, no matter how insincere it may be inside.

# Sense of humour

The constant bombardment on the television of perfectly formed examples of the human race can leave the rest of us mere mortals feeling a little inadequate. However, remember that these people are few and far between and there are other qualities that make people attractive. Apart from obvious physical appearances many women have said that the most attractive thing about a man is his sense of humour, though they might have been joking. If you can make a woman laugh (at your repartee, not at you), it is likely that she will enjoy being with you. This does not mean you need to begin your evening together with a five minute stand up comedy routine combining sharp political satire with quickfire one-liners, but be light-hearted and make witty comments where appropriate.

If she has something serious to say to you, about her problems for instance, be careful not to say something you think is witty and will cheer her up but which she may interpret as insensitive flippancy.

Often the best way to share humour with a girl you don't know very well is to find something (or someone) to laugh at, so that you can share an immediate laugh together. This will be more enjoyable to her than listening to you relating an amusing incident that happened at work yesterday. There may be some incident in a pub, perhaps someone trying to chat-up a girl while holding a copy of this book behind his back.

# Body language - reading the signs

This is one area that requires a least a basic understanding. There have been numerous books published on the intricate subtleties of making sense of eye contact and body postures, knowledge of which is an important tool for first getting to know someone.

We all know a little body language. At its most basic level we know the implicit differences between a smile and a frown, a 'thumbs-up' and a 'thumbs-down' or arms outstretched and arms crossed. These clues enable us to understand a person's emotions or feelings. They make us feel welcome or rejected, happy or sad, without the need for any words to be spoken. We learn these basic rules of body language as we grow up, but in the context of chatting-up the rules and signs are more subtle and intricate and are therefore harder to learn.

Wide, lasting smiles, for instance, are usually more genuine than thin, short ones. A totally limp hand when shaking hands for the first time implies disinterest, while a firm, lingering handshake is a very positive sign. Listen carefully to the tone of her voice: is there a hint

of enthusiasm in it, or does she sound bored?
Watch out also for hidden yawns, heads rolling
to one side, and a blatant unwillingness to enter
your 'personal space'. She may defend her own
personal space by placing her bag between you,
and may demonstrate her unwillingness for
physical contact by keeping her hands in her
pockets. Conversely, if she sits close to you,
moves her hands freely as she talks, and seems
unthreatened and relaxed, she may be opening
up to you. This is not always the case, as some
women act like this with everyone, but you
should at least try to be just as open and relaxed
as she is.

You may boldly smile at a stranger as she passes
you in the street, and she may smile back. It
happens. Her return smile makes her no longer
a stranger. The second time you see her, you
have every right to smile, and the third time you
should stop and say hello, introducing yourself.
All this, and a possible date, can lead from her
initial positive body language. By smiling at this
stranger for the first time, you are telling her
that you find her attractive, and by smiling back
she is returning the compliment. This is no
guarantee of success: she may be flirting for fun,
but that is a risk in any situation. The point is
that you have created another opportunity, and
should act on it without delay provided her
body language is positive.

Eye contact can be just as powerful in telling you not to bother with her. She may glare, look away, or silently mouth something unpleasant. Do not be put off by this, since smiling at a passing girl is very much easier than cold chatting-up, and the rejections are relatively painless. Just keep on looking for the next one to try.

---

**Give her a smile:
this is the simplest way of
'testing the waters'.**

---

*Physical contact*
After you have been chatting for a while, and you believe that she will be receptive to your amorous advances, it is time to think about your first move. This is where a great deal of skill is needed in reading those all important body signals. Unfortunately many people interpret these signals differently. Just because a girl appears to be enjoying your company it does not necessarily mean that she fancies you and wants to kiss you immediately.

Timing is important. Sometimes it is better not to come on too strong at first, in order to avoid seeming desperate. Sometimes, even though you are pretty sure that a girl is interested in you, making that first move is a frightening prospect.

It is not uncommon to leave a date thinking, why on earth did nothing happen? It was usually because making that move seemed impossible. This might have been due to the situation, ie she was with a group of friends, or you just couldn't pluck up the courage. Don't worry: there is usually a next time! Next time you will know better.

'The move' that needs to be made is the action or the words that will make it clear that you want the relationship to be more than platonic. It is tantamount to putting yourself up for sale and asking her if she will buy you. If she doesn't, it means she doesn't want you, and that kind of rejection is never pleasant. In order to minimise the risk of such rejection, men normally wait until they are sure from a woman's body language that she is interested before taking the plunge.

What are the important body language signs that you need to look for? If you are in a room and the girl you are chatting-up seems disinterested when you talk, with her eyes roaming round the room, it would be inadvisable to try to take things further. However, if the girl you are talking to appears to be gazing at you and is not in a hurry to leave the pleasure of your company, then you are probably doing well. The eyes can reveal very much: constant eye contact with you reveals interest in what you are saying. If she looks closely at every other man around, she is less interested. If she looks you up and down continually, this could be a very positive sign. Her mouth provides another clear signal, even if her lips are not mouthing kisses at you. A relaxed smile is clearly positive, a frown is negative. A quick, tight smile every time she realises she has not been paying attention to you is a clear indication of her boredom.

What body signs should you give out yourself? You can kiss her without warning and accept the consequences, or you can test the waters by some gentle physical contact. Hold her hand if you are walking together (take her hand to help her over rough ground or steps, then don't let go), rub her wrist or forearm with your hand or with a stalk of grass if you are lying together sunbathing, or perhaps softly stroke the neck. For the more adventurous, try a quick peck on the cheek, carefully working your way round to the mouth. From there it's easy. This technique is particularly effective during 'slow dances' in nightclubs. If you can get a girl to slow dance with you, you're almost there. Run your fingers firmly up the centre of her back, as far as the back of the neck. If done well, this should generate a feeling similar to a back and neck massage, making her feel warm and comfortable in your hands. Lift her hair with your fingers and gently kiss her neck. If she does not attempt to stop you, work your way round to her mouth with more kisses.

If you want to start with words rather than with actions, you can make it clear that you want to kiss her, either directly or indirectly by asking if she wants to 'come for a walk' etc. Sometimes a girl will make this decision for you, and make the first move. If a girl makes physical contact with you, like touching your hand or even squeezing herself closer to you, these are positive signs and should be acted on.

# Teamwork

If you don't fancy the challenge of going out on your own, the 'my friend fancies you' method can work, believe it or not. This childish approach makes it clear what you want, and if she likes the idea of it there is no messing around with clumsy chat-up before you get it. Best used in nightclubs, parties etc.

More subtle enquiries can yield useful information. A friend can chat to a friend of the girl you are interested in, to find out basic information such as whether she is single, how old she is, does she live locally? You will then be able to begin your chat-up armed with a useful range of conversation topics.

If two of you are on the pull together, finding two unattached females is usually fairly straightforward. Decide in advance who prefers who, then decide on the first chat-up line, such as,

"Didn't I see you at the Selwyn Ball last year?"

You know you didn't, but that doesn't matter. Then start talking. When two of you go for it like this, the confidence level is doubled, the embarrassment level is halved, and you can soon move in and start to talk in pairs rather than as a group of four.

Hunting in threes or more can be much more difficult. Far better to split into smaller groups in order to chat-up smaller groups, otherwise your intimate chat-up lines will be addressed to the whole party.

# Targeting

When there is more than one female available for a potential chat-up, say at a party or nightclub, spend a few minutes deciding which one will offer the best chances. The initial short-list will be dictated by your personal taste: her age, fashion style etc. You must then decide who you have a realistic chance with. If one of them looks like a model, and is flirting with a whole university rugby team, it might be better to aim a little lower. If you are inexperienced and are on a chatting-up mission for the first time, remember you don't learn to drive in a Rolls Royce. Save it until your experience gives you the confidence to go for that sort of person. You won't get the necessary experience, however, if you spend your time asking for driving lessons in that Rolls Royce.

When you have chosen who you want to talk to, and have made the first approach, work on her unless the signs turn negative, then target someone else. Don't keep flogging a dead horse. If she decides she doesn't want to continue chatting you up, it may be because the lights have come back on and she realises that she finds you physically repulsive, or it may be that she is meeting her violently jealous boyfriend in a few minutes and must reluctantly let you go. Forget her. Work on the next one, and keep your options open.

If you are on your own somewhere, you will have little chance of success with a girl who is out with a group of her friends. Better to find someone on her own, though be careful to make sure that she isn't just waiting for her boyfriend to come out of the toilet. If she is with one other friend, it will be awkward for you to chat her up in front of the other. Why not keep the conversation brief, then give her your card and/ or take her number to arrange a later date, provided she seems willing.

If you see someone you like, but do not have the courage or the opportunity to approach her directly, some detective work will be needed to find out her name, and hence her address. Then you can write to her, ring her, or wait to find out a little more about her job or interests to give your letter or phonecall a definite structure.

*Types to go for/avoid*
It should be possible to tell at first glance whether a girl in whom you are interested is likely to be the sort of girl you will have success with. As was mentioned before aim for someone you believe to be of a similar level of attractiveness. Think about the clothes she is wearing, who she is talking to etc. Girls whose dress is very prim and neat, and whose hairstyle

is very conservative, tend to be a little more reserved. While it is not possible to make judgments on a girl's character purely on the basis of the clothes she wears, their whole attitude, from their protective body posture to their clean language, are warning signs that you should read as early as possible. They are often pre-pubescent minds in adult bodies, and will change with experience if you are prepared (or are given the opportunity) to give them that experience.

Girls who dress in a more outrageous manner, who are trying to attract attention by the way they look rather than trying to blend in with the wallpaper, are saying by the way they look, either, 'I'm not a virgin and I'm proud of it,' or, 'I am a virgin but I don't want to be any more.' The choice is yours.

Things to look out for are tight clothes, scruffy clothes, make-up that is aggressive rather than timid, and the general feeling that a great deal of effort has gone into her appearance with the intention of attracting the opposite sex. There are no guarantees, of course, but this could save time in the long run.

Raving feminists are omnipresent. They are harmless really, but need to be tackled with tact if you really want to chat them up.

*Older women*

It is possible that sometimes the woman of your desires is not of your own age. The allure of an older woman is perfectly understandable, though what constitutes older is an entirely relative concept. If you are 14 that could mean a 16 year old. An older woman will often be more experienced, uninhibited and wealthy. Some women get sexier as they mature, others do not stand the test of time so well. It is rare to find someone who is perfectly preserved. For others, features such as laughter lines can drive a man wild. Not everyone finds older women attractive, but it is an experience that is most beneficial, and can be free of many of the problems associated with younger girls. An older woman will usually be less intense and demanding. As they are older they will have had more experience in relationships and will be able to impart to you some of that knowledge.

The issue of children can also enter into the situation. If the woman you are interested in has children you could be letting yourself in for some added difficulties. If the children are young it will mean that she will have more ties and will not have the freedom that you would expect from someone younger.

If the children are older, you could find that they are not overkeen on the thought of you going out with their mother. This is one of the areas where it is not unusual for an older man to go out with a younger woman but if a woman does the same thing it provokes scandal and moral judgement.

*Married women*
Approach with caution: falling for a married woman is very easy, yet it can bring with it many complications. Although many married women are often willing to enter into extra-marital affairs, knowing who they are is not always easy. Many married women often find that after a few years of marriage they need some fresh excitement, and that could be you. It is most likely that this type of indulgence will occur at work. Working companions can often get close to one another, after spending long periods working together. After a while this working relationship can develop into a more personal relationship. This doubles the complications of the relationship, and will more than likely turn your life upside-down before long.

*Young girls*
Youth is a subjective concept, except in the eyes of the law. The age of consent is 16 in Great Britain, and even if you genuinely think she is older but she turns out to be 15, you are committing a criminal offence if you sleep with her. However, a conviction is less likely if the age difference between you is slight. If you are

older than 18, however, the law will expect more restraint from you. The attitude of the girl's parents will often determine what she lets you do, and they are bound to object to their 15 year old going out with a 30 year old, whereas if you are only 16 they should not see any problem.

Other countries have different age laws and attitudes. In some, the age of consent is as low as 12, but you have to be a similar age yourself. An adult could not sleep with a 12 year old, but 13 year old possibly could. The general rule for many places is that a minor can sleep with a minor, a major with a major, but not a major with a minor. What constitutes a major and what a minor can vary, so check your facts if you are worried.

On a practical level, young girls can be less fun in bed, are less interesting to talk to, and have a limited outlook on life. One of the problems commonly found with younger girls is their immaturity. This can lead to periods of sulking, arguing, and irrational behaviour. Trying to reason with a girl of this nature is often futile. It will take many weeks to overcome her sexual inhibitions, during which time you may not even get a decent conversation out of her. It is infuriating, because you know that her next boyfriend will instantly get as much out of her sexually as you did after 6 weeks, but there is no way of speeding up her learning process. If you feel that you are unable to be patient then stick to older girls, but remember that any girl is entitled to decide how ready she is to develop the relationship.

The age gap can also bring other problems such as condemnation from the girl's parents: if you are much older than the girl do not expect them to be overjoyed at the prospect of you going out with their daughter.

*Pretty girls*
Going out with a pretty girl is great for the ego, and is bound to make your friends jealous. So what are the drawbacks? Self-doubt can be a problem. If you are going out with the local sex goddess, you might begin to ask, 'Why is she going out with me, and will it last?' You will have to get used to her having a string of suitors constantly asking her out. This can be very unnerving and demoralising. Another drawback is that sometimes, though not always, a pretty girl will be overconfident and will feel she doesn't need to put in any effort into the relationship. They will be used to not paying, to boyfriends with sports cars and apartments in Paris, and may find your lifestyle does not live up to her expectations.

The implication of all this is that good looking girls are less likely to be faithful to you. True, they are more likely to be given the opportunity to be unfaithful to you, but whether they succumb will depend entirely on the individual.

Many men find the familiar 'blonde bimbo' look appealing. These women, with heavy make-up, dyed hair and carefully chosen clothes, should be avoided unless you consider yourself to be good looking. The fact that they 'tart themselves up' in this way means that appearance is very important to them, and you are more likely to be judged on your looks than on your character. Stick to plainer girls, or girls with more 'original' looks, who may be less narrow minded.

### Not-so-pretty girls

It is true that not every girl is graced with stunning looks and a beautiful body, but accordingly people's tastes vary. We all have our own ideas as to what we believe to be attractive. Don't write off larger women as automatically being unattractive: look for beauty in their face and personality. If you don't like a girl's face very much, look for beauty in her body or her character. If you don't like a girl's body, face or character then leave her alone. The point is, always look for beauty where you may not instinctively search. If you are having trouble chatting-up the sort of women that you regard as the most beautiful in the world for you, try thinking about beauty in another way. Giving different sorts of girls a chance will increase your chances of success and will broaden your life experience.

Unattractive girls can often turn out to be just as sexually experienced as attractive ones. Men are more confident of success when they approach them, they are within everyone's 'league' rather than just in the league of the Chippendales. They also tend to work harder in bed, in an often subconscious effort to compensate for their aesthetic deficiencies by being good lovers. The reverse can be true of attractive girls who feel they don't have to put in any effort in order to 'hook' a man.

As was mentioned earlier in this book beauty is only skin deep and there are far more important qualities that are required for a relationship. In longer relationships you will often see people who are very different in terms of attractiveness: the answer to this is normally that in the long term relationship perhaps the most important factor is that you are best friends. A relationship based on a purely physical basis is often short lived.

*Teacher/student affairs*
Having a crush on your teacher when you were at primary school may have been associated with a Freudian theory of a mothering figure, but as you get older the appeal of a teacher or lecturer can be strong. It is not uncommon to

hear of teachers who give in to the crushes of their students. If you are still at school an affair with a teacher is unlikely, as it is normally the girls that have the affairs with teachers, not pubescent boys. When entering the age of entrance to higher education, however, relationships between lecturers and students become more informal. First names are used and some socialising does occur, and this can lead to the possible development of a relationship.

If you are considering indulging in this type of relationship, be aware of what you are letting yourself in for. This will depend to a large extent on what guise the relationship takes, ie. is it discreet, is the lecturer married? The college authorities take a dim view of lecturers having relationships with their students, and it could lead to a reprimand for the lecturer if you are found out.

So what are the benefits? From a male point of view, it is quite easy to develop a fixation on a lecturer, but much harder to take it beyond that stage. You may be able to arrange private tuition with her, and thus benefit from spending time together without affecting your studies. It will give you a feeling of maturity above your fellow students, you will feel accepted into the 'adult' world of the establishment without the hassle of first having to grow older.

But such relationships are often doomed to secrecy and a feeling of sordidness (nothing wrong with that, you may think). It can be a valuable and mostly enjoyable life experience, but don't expect too much commitment from it.

If you are a teacher or a lecturer, beware! You will be aware to the rules (and of the law in some cases), so tread carefully. You have been warned.

# Sex

Obviously this is a subject to which you will ultimately have to give some thought. This should not be a problem as research has shown that men think about sex far more often than women.

Sex is not necessarily the same as romance. If you are reading this bit because you want to know what it will be like when you eventually get some, you may be in for a shock. Sex is messy, often uncomfortable, funny and rather silly, but it can also be a most beautiful experience. Unless you are very lucky, romantic sex only comes with experience.

If you are inexperienced in these matters, the best approach when you get into bed is to be entirely honest. Some, more experienced women, may find this a real turn on. Or, if you are experienced but are not any good in bed, faking innocence may well get you off the hook. No woman who cares remotely for you will be patronising or unkind if you don't know which hole to aim for or can't put a condom on without reading the instructions on the packet (learn them in advance!) or if you give her a an ice-cream when she asks for a 69. If you don't know what you're doing, say so, make her take things slowly, ask her if she is enjoying what you are doing.

Do not attempt to be too adventurous on your first date. For one, she may not be inclined to be tossed around the bedroom as part of your sexual routine. It is also unwise to unleash the full potential of your sexual repertoire all at once, otherwise she may demand this all the time (what a drag).

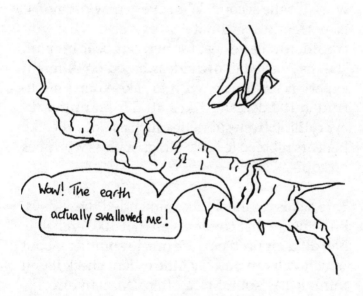

Some girls wanna have fun, others just want to lead you on and then tell you that's it for the night, and can you drive her home? A little sincerity can work wonders, but if it doesn't then you have to play the waiting game. This involves the procedure whereby each time you see her you are allowed to go a little bit further. This type of teasing can often be a challenge, but there are some girls who remain under the impression that virginity is a desirable state (until they finally lose it).

If you have been in a steady relationship for a while, you may find that with someone else the things that turned your first partner on do not work for the second. With every new partner, it is perfectly legitimate to exercise what you consider to be sexiest for her, but bear in mind she may have her own ideas based on different experiences, so it is wise to take your time to find out how she likes it. This applies to everything from subtleties such as does she like her ears nibbled to basic things such as who goes on top?

Safe sex is definitely recommended these days, but beware that condoms are not 100% reliable. Not all their problems are due to splitting, about which you can do very little except check if you think it has split. More often, 'human error' is to blame. The condom may slip off if it has been put on badly or been used for an extended period of time in complicated positions. Of the great variety of condoms available, Durex Gold are a little longer if you want to impress, while ribbed ones are supposed to give extra sensations to the woman.

Non-penetrative sex is a more acceptable alternative these days, and saves money on contraceptives. It can be just as satisfying and sexy as 'doing it', but without the hang-ups and the worry.

Do not feel anxious at the prospect of going to bed with a woman. There is always a mutual feeling of uncertainty and shyness that can make the experience more intimate. For more detail on 'what to do in bed' consult one of the many lovers' handbooks available in book or video form (or ask a friend).

# Love

People say that 'money can't buy love'. We would all like to be rich, but it does not necessarily mean that love will automatically follow (but it is quite likely). It is love that most people are searching for: people need to feel loved as much as they want to love someone.

There are many reasons behind wanting to form a relationship. Ultimately, the question of love enters the brain. But is love at first sight a real phenomenon? You can't really fall in love until you've been out with someone for a while . . . until that point it's called lust, and that is what happens when you first see someone. Lust feels strong, powerful and good, and is very similar to love. But its symptoms are short-lived, real love should last longer.

It is dangerous to fall in love too quickly, anyway. Keep your options open and feelings reserved until you know the girl inside out, otherwise you risk being hurt in an early break-up. There is also the risk of subconsciously applying too much pressure on her to become dedicated to the relationship, and this often leads to rejection on her part.

Love is a powerful emotion causing intense feelings that are not always positive. Crimes of passion are common, often due to jealously or betrayal. The destructive powers of love are frightening and therefore when falling in love it must always be remembered that apart from happiness it can bring sadness and despair. Many people deliberately avoid falling in love just to avoid the complications it can bring and the unhappiness that replaces it when a relationship is over. It is rare to be happier after an unsuccessful relationship than you were before. But the maxim, 'it is better to have loved and lost than never to have loved at all' is true: even if you are unhappier after the relationship, it is rare to regret that the relationship ever happened. Don't be put off; in general love is the ultimate experience and can end in happy marriage.

*Soul mates*
What's love got to do with it? What is love? Where do I find love? We spend our lives searching for love, perhaps without ever thinking about what we are really looking for. The majority of people are attempting to find contentment and fulfilment in a relationship. This ideal unfortunately appears to be hard to achieve.

The ultimate relationship could be based on the finding of a 'soul mate'. This expression is often referred to as 'twin soul'. A soul mate is like the other half of yourself: the minute you set eyes on that person you know they are 'the one', and that a union of the two halves will bring a wholeness to you that is seldom otherwise achieved.

Some people are constantly searching for their soul mate and will not settle for less, believing that somewhere out there is a perfect partner for them. This is a beautiful notion and one that I believe to be true; the only flaw is that, assuming your soul mate is unique in the world, finding her is about as likely as finding palm trees in Alaska.

What is more likely is that within every group of, say, a thousand people, there will be several potential soul mates for each person. You can never say that a particular girl is 'the only girl in the world for me, no one else could make me this happy.' That is not true, even though it probably seems to be true. No one can possibly become acquainted with more than the tiniest fraction of the world's population, and while no two people are identical, there are probably hundreds of thousands of women who possess the similar physical and mental characteristics to your 'one and only'. Had your life taken a slightly different course, you would have been just as happy with any one of them.

Meeting, dating and marrying is so full of random chance as to whom you encounter and finally marry that it is nothing but romantic hyperbole to say that any individual is the best in the world. There are so many women who could fulfil the role of soul mate that your chances of finding one on your 'random' journey through life are actually very good, provided you don't hide yourself away from human contact. So don't worry: when someone says that the girl for you is out there, somewhere, don't take it literally. The girl for you is any one of hundreds of thousands of girls, all of whom could be equally suited, and at least one of whom you are bound to meet.

# How to write a love letter

The practice of letter writing is a dying art form, which is a shame because although using other media of communication such as the telephone obviously requires less effort, receiving a telephone call does not have the same satisfaction as receiving a letter. The only letters that most of us write are to bank managers and these are rarely of a romantic nature. Sending a letter shows the girl that you are making an effort and she should be impressed, especially as it is now such a rarity.

A love letter does not have to be filled with romantic slobbering. You could be writing just to thank for her the pleasure of her company, or to tell her you think she's wonderful. Flattery without obsequiousness is probably the best tone to aim for.

A letter can also be used as an alternative to approaching a girl for the first time directly. This can either be from cold, ie. a letter to a girl that you know but who doesn't know you, telling her you have seen her around and would like to meet her, or a letter as a romantic follow up to a date or a meeting, perhaps accompanied by flowers or chocolates. In either case, be mildly flattering, but not over the top. Be light-hearted and witty, not morbidly serious about your undying love for her.

If literary greatness is not your scene, don't use a large, blank piece of paper, just write on the back of an arty postcard or a small sheet of writing paper. With letters, it is much harder to avoid talking about yourself than it is in conversation, since a page of questions about her will look more like an exam than a love letter. The best approach is to concentrate on things you have done together, if any, or refer to things you have in common. Failing that, write about something you would like to do with her (apart from . . .)

Romantic notes can now be sent by more modern methods: messages of love sent by fax or by computer electronic mail can add spice to office relationships and are still relatively innovative means of saying what you want to say. The combination of old fashioned writing skills with modern technology is sure to impress.

# How to write a love poem

This is best avoided unless you know what you are doing. A really bad poem is unlikely to be of any help to you. But if you want to give it a try, a good approach is to make it sound grand and stylish. To achieve this, use lots of classical imagery. Drop in names of Greek and Roman classical gods, and compare the girl's attributes to the levels of perfection personified by such gods.

There is nothing wrong with taking a famous poem and adapting it to your own needs, replacing the name of the poet's loved one with that of yours. As with letter writing, a girl will normally be very impressed if you try to write a poem especially for her. It is the thought that counts, and she will not expect you to be the next poet Laureate. Expressing your feelings in this form might be an easier way of letting her know how you feel about her than if you actually had to tell her directly.

The following poem, 'Flavours', manages to maintain a light-hearted tone whilst saying to the girl that she is very special to the poet. It is

romantic, but in a gentle sense, without forcing
the poet's love too strongly upon the recipient.

**Flavours**

The weight of a cacophony of feelings
Bends me like a spoon,
Scooping for love here and there,
And filling slowly without satisfaction.
There are many flavours
In the frozen compartment of winter:
Exotic fruits and sweet tangs,
Vanilla ice and coconut;
But all are cold and hard,
Encased in snow.
There is but one flavour that warms me,
That melts the winter ice
And sits gently on the spoon,
Happy and kind,
Smiling at the absurdities of life,
Conquering the fears and the strains
That pressure me,
Soothing like and Ovaltinee,
And comforting like a sofa.
It is a flavour more delicious
Than chocolate, more tantalising
Than the secrets of the stars,
And more full than Mr Branson's
Bank account. It is a flavour
I have found nowhere else
In this wild and incomprehensible world,
And I am glad. My spoon is full
And I am content and the flavour
Is you.

The second poem is written by Andrew Marvell, and is a little more direct in its approach. The woman he is trying to go to bed with wants to take things slowly and to retain her purity; he argues, what is the point? We'll all be dead soon, so why not enjoy our bodies while we can?

**To His Coy Mistress**

Had we but world enough, and time,
This coyness, Lady, were no crime.
We would sit down and think which way
To walk and pass our long love's day.
Thou by the Indian Ganges' side
Shouldst rubies find: I by the tide
Of Humber would complain. I would
Love you ten years before the Flood,
And you should, if you please, refuse
Till the conversion of the Jews.
My vegetable love should grow
Vaster than empires, and more slow;
An hundred years should go to praise
Thine eyes and on thy forehead gaze;
Two hundred to adore each breast;
But thirty thousand to the rest;
An age at least to every part,
And the last age should show your heart;
For, Lady, you deserve this state,
Nor would I love at lower rate.
But at my back I always hear
Time's winged chariot hurrying near;

And yonder all before us lie
Deserts of vast eternity.
Thy beauty shall no more be found,
Nor, in thy marble vault, shall sound
My echoing song: then worms shall try
That long preserved virginity,
And your quaint honour turn to dust
And into ashes all my lust:
The grave's a fine and private place,
But none, I think, do there embrace.
Now therefore, while the youthful hue
Sits on thy skin like morning dew,
And while thy willing soul transpires
At every pore with instant fires,
Now let us sport us while we may,
And now, like amorous birds of prey,
Rather at once our time devour
Than languish in his slow-chapt power.
Let us roll all our strength and all
Our sweetness up into one ball,
And tear our pleasures with rough strife
Thorough the iron gates of life:
Thus, though we cannot make our sun
Stand still, yet we will make him run.

If writing a poem like that does not appeal to you, why not copy out any classic love poem that says what you want to say? Summersdale has published the perfect anthology for this purpose: **Classic Love Poems**, (ISBN 1 873475 500), available from all good bookshops.

# Spending money

Chatting-up inevitably involves spending money at some point. It can become an expensive pastime unless you apply a degree of self-control over how much you spend on someone before getting anywhere. Don't shower her with flowers and gifts right from the start. You'll appear too keen and she will feel under pressure and will sense your desperation to keep her. (This is not a problem if she is as desperate as you are.) Buy a drink at a bar, if you want, but why not be different and ask her to buy you a drink? If it works you might score at her expense, which is surely the pinnacle of achievement?

These days, many women will probably insist on either paying for the meal themselves, or at least paying for their share of it. Unless you are very much wealthier than her, don't protest too much at such an offer. Women have pride too. Some women will find a man who makes a big deal of telling her how much money he is spending on her a real turn off. In terms of spending money a girl does not normally equate how much a person spends to how wonderful he is, it is the thought that counts. However, this does not mean that if you are thinking of taking her out to dinner, you take her to a hamburger bar.

# How to act in front of her parents

Meeting a girl's parents for the first time can be a harrowing experience. You will never be good enough for their daughter, so the tradition goes, so you will have to be on your best behaviour if you want them to grant a reluctant approval. You may not care about this, but some girls actually listen to their parents' advice and opinions, so it may be in your own interest to make an effort.

Some parents need treating with kid gloves. They will be keen to know what line of work you are in, what your prospects are, and what university you went to. If you envisage a short relationship, lie to them to your heart's content. Otherwise, don't mention that you are currently on parole for assault, just tell them what you would like to do, career wise. 'I'm thinking of doing a CPE to become a lawyer,' does not require any action or ability, since you will never do it, but they don't need to know that.

Nicer, down-to-earth parents are not usually a problem at all. They will not interfere in their daughter's love life, and will hopefully welcome you into the family for the time you are there.

When staying at a girlfriend's house while her parents are there, the main problem is that of sleeping arrangements. If you want to stay on good terms with her parents, it is best to respect their wishes, no matter how unreasonable. You may have spent ninety-nine out of a hundred nights at college sharing a single bed with her, but at her house you will not be allowed within a mile of her double bed. If you don't have any respect for her parents, this won't be a problem as there is always the option of sneaking into her room at night provided the floorboards and bedsprings are quiet enough.

# When things turn sour . . .

Although romance can bring much joy and happiness it can also bring with it some unpleasantness. First impressions can be misleading, and if the girl of your dreams turns out after a few dates to be mildly less interesting than Radio 3 on a quiet night, you will need to break it to her that you don't want to continue the relationship. At this early stage, breaking off should be relatively painless. Her emotional attachment will not be too strong, and you will either hurt her pride a little or make her relieved that she didn't have to chuck you herself. A phonecall will suffice, saying you have enjoyed your time together, but that you don't think it is really working, or that your old girlfriend has asked you back and you found it hard to refuse.

Breaking up after the relationship has become properly established is, of course, more difficult and potentially fraught with problems. If it is to be done suddenly, you should see her in person and break it to her gently, with an opportunity for her to cry on your shoulder if necessary. A letter or a phonecall in this instance can be rather cruel, but there is no way of avoiding pain with any method.

If possible, go for the 'trial separation' approach. Suggest that you feel you need some time to yourself, if only a week or so, and that you will review your feelings then. This will give her advance warning of the split, and will lessen the shock when it comes.

"some women react very badly to splitting up."

Some women react very badly after splitting up. However rational you believe she might have been, this could well disappear after you have ended the relationship. You might have to face a vendetta that will either make you thankful that you ended this now or make you wonder when the next plane is leaving for Rio. A girl that has been dumped can slag you off to her friends and possibly your friends. The best way to deal with a difficult and often painful situation is to avoid her as much as possible.

If you are ending a long term relationship where you have been living together this can cause even more problems. The arguments over possessions, who is going to move out, etc, can turn faded love into fiery hate. The thought of this kind of hassle is sometimes enough to make people continue in the relationship for the sake of a quiet life. If you are certain that you are not happy in a long-term relationship, it is best to get out of it as soon as possible. The longer it is left, the harder it is to do. The next thing you know, you are standing at the altar with a girl who you probably don't want to marry.

# Astrology

Your destiny lies in your own hands, right? Or
does it? Some may regard it as mumbo jumbo,
but there appears to be an increasing fascination
with astrology. Star signs, sun signs etc. are all
said to be connected to our behaviour.

We are all probably familiar with basic signs of
the zodiac. Leo, Capricorn, Pisces etc and the
characteristics that are associated with our own
sign. But what are the characteristics of other
signs? If you believe in them, they could be of
use in deciding whether a particular woman is
for you or not, and even if you don't believe in
them you will at least be armed with a
conversational topic that is of interest to many
women.

## Capricorn
(23rd December - 20th January)
*The goat*

Capricorns are stable and dependable. They are perfectionists with ambition and determination, often critical of others but over-confident of their own abilities. Their emotions are moderate.

## Aquarius
(21st January - 19th February)
*The water carrier*

Aquarians are individualists, often becoming eccentric. Absent-minded and detached, they also possess vision and genius. They have the power of persuasion with their pleasant manner, though they can also be stubborn.

## Pisces
(20th February - 20th March)
*The fish*

Pisceans are generous in love, sensitive and sympathetic. While they can be compassionate, they can also be shy, nervous and easily led.

## Aries
(21st March - 20th April)
*The ram*

Arians are vivacious, sparkling and headstrong. A fiery temper coupled with impulsiveness is their downside, but courage, a strong work ethic and an ability to inspire others are their positive qualities.

## Taurus
(21st April - 21st May)
*The bull*

Taurans are practical people. They see what they want and go for it, no matter what the obstacles. Strong willed and independent, they can also be stubborn and unreasonable.

## Gemini
(22nd May - 21st June)
*The twins*

Geminians are quick thinking, versatile and unpredictable. They are good talkers and make friends easily, but can be shallow, unreliable and impatient.

## Cancer
(22nd June - 23rd July)
*The crab*

An ambitious sign: Cancerians who can harness their emotions can become great achievers. They possess imaginative, bold minds, hampered only by moodiness, sensitivity and caution.

## Leo
(24th July - 23rd August)
*The lion*

Leo people possess powers of influence and leadership, coupled with generosity and a sense of romance. However, they can be oppressive, patronising and over-exuberant.

## Virgo
(24th August - 23rd September)
*The virgin*

Bright, realistic thinkers, Virgo people are polite, sensible and adaptable. But they can also be critical of others, pessimistic and a little odd.

## Libra
(24th September - 23rd October)
*The scales*

Librans possess a sense of justice, and though intelligent they are often easily influenced. Their emotional 'scales' may be well balanced, but they can be lazy and indecisive.

## Scorpio
(24th September - 22nd November)
*The scorpion*

Scorpions are strong willed, self controlled and powerful. They can make of lot of friends with their magnetism, but must control their unsympathetic, suspicious and cruel traits.

## Sagittarius
(23rd November - 22nd December)
*The archer*

Sagittarians possess honesty, enthusiasm and high standards. They can be bold and cheerful as well as reckless, blunt and miserly.

*There are certain star signs that are believed to be better matched than others. These are:*

**Capricorn**- Virgo, Aries, Taurus, Cancer

**Aquarius** - Gemini, Virgo, Leo, Libra

**Pisces** - Cancer, Scorpio, Virgo, Taurus

**Aries** - Gemini, Leo, Sagittarius, Capricorn

**Taurus** - Virgo, Scorpio, Capricorn, Pisces

**Gemini** - Libra, Aquarius, Aries, Sagittarius

**Cancer** - Libra, Scorpio, Capricorn, Pisces

**Leo** - Aries, Sagittarius, Aquarius, Scorpio

**Virgo** - Taurus, Aquarius, Capricorn, Pisces

**Libra** - Aquarius, Sagittarius, Gemini, Cancer

**Scorpio** - Cancer, Taurus, Pisces, Leo

**Sagittarius** - Leo, Aries, Gemini, Libra

Using star signs to match compatibility is all very well but you could be avoiding some girls just because the 'stars' advise that you are not well matched. Individuals vary greatly in their personal characteristics, even when they share the same birthday, so give everyone a chance before ruling them out. Although it might be sexist to say so, the greatest interest in astrology tends to lie with women. Even if you consider it to be a load of baloney, if a woman is convinced purely by her stars that you and she are incompatible, you have a serious problem unless you can persuade her that you do not fit the characteristics that she would like to avoid.

If you believe in astrology there is a danger that relying on the stars and various charts can rule your life. There are, of course, always believers and non-believers. Skeptics argue that the advice is normally so vague that it could easily be applied to anyone. For instance, if it said you are likely to meet a tall dark haired girl whilst shopping, well even the most reckless bookmaker would not take bets on this event occurring. People often read it how they want to see it.

# SCENARIOS
# Bar/pub

Although the good old English pub has traditionally been associated with pulling, it is often the hardest place to succeed. Approaching a girl in a pub, especially if you are on your own and she is with a group of girls, takes more balls than a Bingo machine. If the pub is sufficiently crowded, you can approach one member of a group on her way to or from the bar, but in an otherwise empty pub you will be seen and laughed at by her friends. She will then feel self conscious, and will not respond positively to your approach.

Choosing your pub is easy in your home town. There will usually be one for students, one for under age drinkers, and one for single people. Avoid one that has a good reputation for darts and billiards. Go for something crowded where there is no room for sitting down, which gives you the freedom to circulate and to get close to a girl in a subtle manner. Excessive noise from a band or a juke box can make chatting-up difficult, but at least you won't have to say anything more adventurous than monosyllables.

The pub is often a good stepping stone to somewhere a little more interesting, like her bedroom or the beach. Don't spend too much money on alcohol in the pub if you have a bottle of wine at home and expect her to come home with you soon. If appropriate, explain that funds are low but that there is plenty of wine in your house, and hope that she doesn't simply offer to buy the next round.

# Nightclub

A good, busy club can be paradise for picking up girls. Little chat is required, due to the noise level, so often all you will have to do is to shout the first line, either asking her to dance or offering to buy her a drink, which is all you can do there anyway, then dance or drink with her until the slow dances. Once your octopus arms have surrounded her on the dance floor, run your fingers up her spine to the neck, pressing hard for a massage effect. Kiss her neck, then her cheek, then the lips, all the time remembering to keep those feet shuffling around a little, as it is meant to be a dance.

In this respect it is like being abroad, where physical attraction is enough, and there is no need to be witty or eloquent. If good looks are not your forte, the nightclub environment helps in that the flashing lights and misty atmosphere can improve most people's appearance.

Some nightclubs are known as cattle markets, due to the ease with which anyone can 'score'. Some even have rows of girls in stilettos lined against the wall waiting to be asked to dance. Very little finesse in chatting-up is called for here, but such encounters are unlikely to lead to a fulfilling relationship.

If loud music and bright lights create the right environment to make you feel at home when chatting-up, then nightclubs are for you. It may sound obvious, but remember that the type of girl you are likely to meet there will be the type of girl who goes to nightclubs.

# Street

The street is an environment in which the eye contact techniques and smiling can be used to great effect. It works on strangers and on people you know to some degree. Breaking the ice with a smile can lead to positive feedback; maybe not instantly, but perhaps the next time you meet in that street.

Be prepared for these chance encounters at any time. If you are just popping out to the shops for a carton of milk, make sure you are looking your best. It is at times when you are looking your worst, in your most unflattering gardening clothes, that you are likely to meet the girl of your dreams and not be ready for her. That's Sod's Law and you have to expect it.

# Introductions

One of the biggest stumbling blocks to successfully chatting-up a stranger is the mood of fear that is often prevalent today. It is natural to be suspicious of someone you don't know, and even an evening's discussion may not sufficiently dispel her fears to make her want to go home with you or give you her telephone number.

Every woman likes to feel that the man she is talking to has been 'vetted' in some way, that he is an established friend of someone she already knows, and is not a maniac newly arrived in town and about to clear out after his next attack. For this reason introductions by friends, however informal, are worth their weight in gold. A glowing character reference from a mutual friend can send a relationship into orbit that would have otherwise fizzled out on the launch pad. Make the most of introductions wherever possible, ask a friend to introduce you to someone you have seen them with and who you would like to get to know. At the very least, you can find out from your friend whether that girl is single or is likely in any way to be interested.

Dating agencies also provide a degree of

'screening' of clients. They can match you with potential partners who possess similar interests and characteristics, thus removing the huge 'random' element that is otherwise prevalent when chatting-up. This random element normally dictates that a great many of the people you meet will not be 'suitable' for you, or will not even be looking for a relationship at all. Using an agency is a more precise, efficient way of chatting-up: at least you know that she really is single when you meet in this way. Why not try one of the agencies advertised in the back of this book?

*Interview with Hillie Marshall of Dinner Dates*

*Q     Hillie Marshall, you run a company called Dinner Dates. Can you tell us about it?*

**A**     Dinner Dates is a dining and social events club for single people. The dinner parties are held in the best restaurants, hotels and private members nightclubs in London and South East England, including Claridges, The Ritz, Richard Branson's Kensington Roof Gardens, Mortons, The Elephant on the River and The Park Lane Hilton. The evenings start with a drinks reception where all the guests, usually sixteen men and sixteen women of similar ages and interests, are introduced to each other. At dinner guests are seated at tables of eight with placecards, and after the main course the men change places to pre-assigned seats on the other table in their group so there is a new set of people to talk to. After dinner they can dance or mingle and chat till the early hours.

The next day we have a follow up service when we telephone everyone to ask how they enjoyed themselves and also enquire if there is anyone they might like to contact if they haven't made their own arrangements. If there is we contact the other person and if they are agreeable we phone back with the telephone number.

We also arrange group activity holidays including ski chalet trips, tennis and golf weekends, clay pigeon shooting, paintballing, treasure hunts, theatre evenings, murder mystery evenings and special events such as Royal Ascot, Henley Royal Regatta, Cowdray Park Polo and Glorious Goodwood. There is always plenty to do each week.

*Q    What sort of people come to Dinner Dates and why?*

**A**    Perfectly normal people from all walks of life who want to widen their circle of friends, and maybe meet someone who will be special to them. You certainly won't increase your chances of meeting that person by sitting at home eating baked beans and watching the television! Dinner Dates members are people who have decided to do something about their lives and not sit around waiting for life to come to them.

Q   *Why is there a need for organisations such as yours?*

A   Nowadays people tend to work long and unsociable hours in order to secure their jobs, and delay thinking about settling down with a partner. They reach an age where maybe their friends are married and don't have single friends to introduce them to, which they might have had in their teens and twenties. They have left behind the world of being picked up in wine bars, pubs and clubs, which is dangerous anyway, and are more discerning about who they would like to meet.

We provide an initial point of contact in a congenial atmosphere with no pressure whatsoever, and members who come to our functions with an open mind, no pre-conceived ideas, and are fun people that everyone would like to be with, invariably land up meeting that special person for them.

Q   *You must have observed hundreds of men chatting-up women at your events and also been told a lot about what goes on. Can you give us some tips?*

A   Yes, you're right. We have over six

thousand members and during the six years I have been running Dinner Dates I have gained quite a bit of knowledge.

First of all a man must show interest in the woman he is chatting-up. If he likes her appearance, her clothes, even her perfume then he should tell her. Don't give false flattery that anyone can see through, but genuinely make her feel good.

Find out what interests her and be a good listener. There is nothing worse than a man who talks non-stop about himself, his likes and dislikes, as this may indicate to the woman being chatted-up that he may not at a later date be bothered about pleasing her and satisfying her needs.

He should give her his full attention - women do not like talking to men whose eyes are looking everywhere except at them!

Concentrate on what she says as it is very unflattering later in the conversation when a question is repeated, indicating that the man has not been giving her his undivided attention. This behaviour certainly led to a disastrous situation one night at Dinner Dates. A man had been chatting-up a particular woman all evening and finally feeling he was on safe ground he asked for her telephone number. She said,

"No!"

"Why?" he asked.

"You sat next to me in this same restaurant last year and asked for my phone number. I gave it to you and you still haven't rung me!" she replied.

Try not to ask too many questions to start with like, "What do you do?" or, "Where do you live?" Don't try to pigeonhole a woman, it makes her freeze.

A sense of humour is absolutely essential, and trying to generate humour relaxes the woman as well as making her laugh.

Always be positive - a negative and complaining attitude is a complete turn-off. Also, don't mention your problems causing her attention to wander as she probably has enough of her own!

To my mind, single people should throw away their check-lists about the perfect person they would like to meet. This being does not exist. If, during the conversation, a woman feels the man is ticking off various points on a mental check-list, she will run a mile.

Having chatted-up the lady in question and decided that he would like to ask her out, the next big hurdle is to get her telephone number. If he feels nervous about a possible rejection he could try a novel way round the problem. One of my members has found a foolproof method. He asks the woman to write her signature for him; he tells her how interesting it is and says he is into graphology and would like to do her signature analysis. He has a special computer programme for this and if she would like to give him her telephone number they can meet when he has completed it, and give her the results. This approach never fails! Women can't wait to receive the results and this also provides a wonderful conversation piece at their next meeting.

Q    *Thank you Hillie Marshall of Dinner Dates.*

# Parties

Chatting-up at a party is in many ways one of the most likely routes to success. Talking to someone you don't know at a party is not as difficult as talking to a stranger elsewhere, since you have a friend in common, ie the host of the party. It is also likely that you will have other friends in common, and this should be your starting topic of conversation.

Parties in private houses are better than in rented halls or rooms because they offer so many intimate corners and cupboards that can encourage the shedding of inhibitions. You can go for a moonlit stroll in the garden, or explore the cellar where the light is conveniently not working. In a rented hall there are no intimate corners, the room is one large square and everyone can see where you are all the time.

One of the best places to get talking to a girl is on the stairs, or at the top of the stairs while she is queuing to use the toilet. You must, of necessity, get close to each other in order to let others pass by, and you are generally less on view than in a room. The best sort of approach for an opening line in this instance is the 'Aren't you a friend of . . .' line of attack, which not only gets her thinking but shows that you have at least one friend. While you will not (hopefully) have to buy her a drink, you can offer her some of your stash of better quality wine that you brought with you and hid behind some books. It is always good to be able to share something early on, to give yourselves the tiniest sense of a joint identity. She will be able to accept you more quickly as a friend in this way.

# Office

Relationships at work can be politically complicated, and are best avoided. Your working relationship with someone can be affected if you become ex-lovers, or your promotion may be seen in an unfavourable light by your colleagues if you have slept with your female boss.

If she is just someone else in your department, that will cause fewer problems, but may still present difficulties with the other staff. There will always be the suspicion that when the two of you are together during working hours you will be doing anything but working, and if your boss thinks this then you had better be careful.

The greatest temptations and opportunities come at office parties. When people you work with all year round let their hair down, it can be one of society's wildest events. If an office relationship is what you really want, this is the time to go for it.

However, when everyone knows each other this well, inhibitions are stronger and no one is going to want to be seen 'forming a new relationship' publicly in front of all their colleagues. Make sure the woman you are with is away from her closest colleagues before you make a move. If possible, find somewhere completely private. Then, at least, you have the option of keeping the 'occurrence' secret.

# Holidays

Chatting-up abroad is far easier than at home. People on holiday are more laid back, stress free and more open to exciting ideas such as skinny-dipping. Chatting-up foreign girls is the easiest thing in the world, and is the best way to build up your confidence if you haven't had much luck in Blighty. Where there is a language barrier, chatting-up becomes much easier. You are not expected to say anything cool or clever, and only the barest of platitudes need be exchanged before you can get down to kissing her. Without talking, your communication is of a much more physical nature, so you are more likely to get straight to physical activities than if you had to spend half the night trying to convince her you were a green vegetarian before she would let you sleep with her.

Some package holidays are designed for getting laid. Destinations such as Ibiza, Greece, and the Spanish coast have all the tacky nightclub facilities suitable for this purpose. However, most young Britons tend to go to these places for the same reason that you might go there, so for less competition why not try the South of France, Italy or even Holland or Denmark?

Take a good supply of condoms on holiday, just in case. Foreign ones may not be so easy to come by. Also, you are more likely to get a chance to use them in some countries than in others. Remember that some countries are deeply religious, and while Spanish girls may look appealing, many have a severely limited sexual repertoire outside of marriage. For greater liberation, look to girls from northern Europe who have some pretty advanced ideas and attitudes towards sex. Don't regard this advice as being a hard and fast rule, of course, but be aware of the general trends that exist.

# Swimming

As was mentioned earlier, no opportunity should be missed. If you see a girl you fancy and it happens to be in a swimming pool, you could be missing out on the girl of your dreams if you decide not to make any attempt. As with the gym, swimming involves exposing your flesh to all. Many people feel uncomfortable, thinking they are too fat, too thin or lacking the healthy glow of a Mediterranean tan, but this must not be allowed to hinder your confidence, as previously mentioned. In the long term you may be able to do something about it, but for now just think positive or put a T-shirt on.

It is possible to strike up a conversation with a girl at the ends of the pool, especially if you are swimming lengths and you pass that person several times. I think that pretending to drown in the hope of being rescued by a beautiful girl is a little on the drastic side, and you would probably be rescued by an old lady, who would try to give you the kiss of life. If you have managed to make eye contact whilst swimming, then you might bump into her after getting changed. There is no harm in asking if she fancies a drink.

If you are working with someone who you fancy, try casually mentioning you are going swimming. If she expresses any interest, ask if she would like to come. The suggestion to go swimming might seem less threatening than asking her out for a date, though she may not feel happy about being seen in her swimming costume on a first date.

Suppose you have been 'successfully' chatting someone up all evening, the pub is about to close, and you're stuck for ideas as to what to do next. Why not take her to the local lake/river/beach for a midnight swim? Find somewhere private and not too polluted to ensure an evening of romance and excitement. She may object to the idea on the grounds of having no towel, but you can counter that by ensuring that you always carry a towel in the car.

# Clubs and societies

If you are single and your circle of immediate friends is not large enough to bring you into contact with new faces with any regularity, joining a local club or society can be a great way to meet someone. Look in your local paper for a list of societies and when they meet, and go to a meeting to see what it's like. These societies are always keen for new members and will always give you a chance. If there is no one there who appeals to you, try another interest. Once you find someone, getting to know them will be far easier than if you were not sharing that special interest with her. The club will give you an instant topic of conversation, shared experience and mutual friends to talk about.

Typical clubs might include drama societies, local interest groups, politics, photography, film, art, rambling and other outdoor pursuits. Join a sports centre by all means, but joining a club dedicated to one particular sport may be a waste of time if no women are involved.

# The gym

If you look like Mr Puniverse and you have trouble lifting a bag of sugar, impressing the girls with your pectorals is definitely a no-no. Always keep yourself covered up: you are more likely to score if you can give the impression that you are fit and healthy. Wear a sweat shirt that covers either your skinny ribs or hides your flab.

The girls that tend to hang out at gyms can range from the stunning, toned, usually tanned to the type that can bend steel bars between their teeth. The latter should be avoided; a rejection from this type might land you in hospital for six weeks.

Getting fit, or for most of us losing weight is the primary reason for all that pain and suffering usually inflicted during a serious workout. But why do we want to lose weight? Because we want to be more attractive to women. The sight of a flabby stomach is often enough to cool the ardour of most women. This can be cured by consistent and careful dieting, regular sit-ups, and occasional jogging. Once you have a woman then you can revert back to gluttony.

Trying to score in a gym is not easy, but if you want to be successful with women no opportunity should be missed. Another life saving tip: when chatting-up some gorgeous girl on the next exercise bike, be warned that the gorilla opposite lifting half a ton might be her boyfriend.

Even if you don't actually manage to pull in the gym, working out regularly will increase your chances of pulling in other scenarios.

# Library

If you are a student, you may be aware that your college has a library. Ask someone to tell you where it is, then go along with some books and a pen and seat yourself in view of some swotty, but pretty, girls, and pretend to work. The library has its own unique atmosphere, which engenders a sense of boredom and desperation in those who frequent it, so most girls there will be pleased to be distracted by you. Make eye contact with someone you like, and remember where they are seated. If you go to the library often you will find that most girls sit in roughly the same seat every day or every evening, and if you regularly sit near to them they will get to recognise and know you. From that stage it can be possible to break for lunch at the same time as them, or to walk them home, perhaps asking for shelter under her umbrella if it's raining (girls who live in libraries are very sensible and are bound to have an umbrella). The library is not a hunting ground that will give you an instant result, but given time you can develop some meaningful relationships.

Non-students can also use this approach either in a public library or in a student library if they can dress scruffily enough to pass as a student and get in.

# Supermarket

It has happened to all of us, well, probably: one minute you were trying to decide whether to pick up the frozen peas or a pack of pizzas, the next minute your eyes meet with a woman who is fondling a bag of halibut. It's love at first sight, but what do you do? The best approach is to talk about something which is appropriate to the situation in which you both find yourselves. A question about cookery is a good start.

"Can you microwave this?"

Another tactic is the accidental trolley bump. This never fails to attract the attention of the object of your desire. Be careful not to nudge too hard.

Detective work can pay dividends here. Observe what is in her basket or trolley. The contents can give clues to her marital status etc. If she has children, you will see lots of dinosaur drinks, mini mars bars and nappies. What you want to see are ready made meals for one.

Try to queue with her at the checkout, helping her lift heavy items from the trolley, if it is possible to do so without seeming too sexist or patronising. Chat to her about her food, cookery and the weather.

If there is a cashier that appeals to you, use her checkout every week until she knows you. Start with a simple,

"Hello again,"

progressing to,

"How are you today?"

After a few weeks, try a full conversation. Finally, ask when she finishes and tell her you'll be in the pub from 9.00 pm until 10.00 pm and that she is welcome to join you for a drink if she wants to unwind after working so hard.

# Public transport

Just because you are sitting on a train commuting to work does not mean you should not try chatting someone up. Face to face train seats are ideal for this, and you may have anything up to several hours of pleasant chat with her before her stop. If starting conversations is difficult, why not help her lift her bag up to the luggage rack, saying,

"Can I help you with that?"

It is a little sexist these days, but she will more often than not be grateful. Once started, talk about British Rail, the wrong type of snow, things you pass, plus of course her job, her town and her reason for this trip. Try for a full character study before she leaves. At this point it is always important to produce a card if you want to have even the remotest chance of seeing her again. This can apply to any form of public transport. Say something like,

"I don't normally do this sort of thing, but here's my card - I'd like to keep in touch if possible."

Make the card look scruffy and hard to find in your wallet so that she does not think that you do this all the time.

# A - Z of chat-up lines:

## *A:*

Are you alright? *(If she is on her own and appears to be upset or just quiet. Can follow with asking about her problems, listening sympathetically, then giving her a cuddle.)*

Am I right in thinking you're . . .'s friend?

Aren't you a friend of . . . ?

Asking you for a date: would that be a waste of time?

Are you a fan of . . . ?

Afternoon. How are you?

## *B:*

Bloody hell, watch where you're going! *(As she bumps into you. You can then apologise and offer to make it up to her with a drink later.)*

Before I buy you a drink, can you tell me your name? *(If you're feeling cocky).*

Believe me, I've tried to come up with a really

original chat-up line: it's very hard, but as I'm now talking to you and you know why, I might as well carry on.

# C:

Can I buy you a drink? *(One of the all time favourites, yet doesn't appear too clichéd. Definitely worth trying once you've made eye contact.)*

Can you microwave this? *(Supermarkets)*

Can I help you with that? *(Heavy shopping etc)*

Could you help me with this, please? *(Role reversal)*

Can you tell me the time, please? *(Hide your watch first).*

Can you help me out? I need a dinner date this week.

Could you recommend a good chat-up line? *(Repeat whatever she says.)*

# D:

Do you come here often? *(Never to be used.)*

Don't drink the beer here. It's awful. Try . . . instead.

Do you fancy having dinner next week?

Do you know a good Italian restaurant nearby?
*(If she replies 'yes' ask if she would like to go there.)*

Do you like my new jacket/car *etc*?

Do you want to hear my best chat-up line? *(She
says, 'OK', you reply, 'That was it'.)*

Didn't I see you here last week/month?

# *E:*

Every time I come here I've seen you. What's
your name?

Er, hello. My name's . . .

Evening. How are you?

Everyone says you *(were in the local paper this
week / are the barman's daughter / work in an
abattoir)* . . . is this true? Tell me about it.

Each time I see you I tell myself I'm going to
talk to you, and now I've finally done it.

# *F:*

Fancy a swim? *(Useful if you have your own pool*

*or if you are on holiday near the sea or a lake. Great*
*excuse for skinny dipping, otherwise known as*
*inspecting the goods before you buy.)*

Forgive me for being so forward, but may I
introduce myself?

# G:

Got a light?

Going so soon? Stay a minute and let me get
you a drink.

# H:

Hi there. *(Can also say Hello if being more formal.*
*Usually follow with introducing yourself and small*
*chat.)*

Hello. What's your name?

How would you like your eggs in the morning?
*(She will reply, 'Unfertilised, please.')*

Have you got a problem with that? *(Broken down*
*car, chain loose on bicycle etc)*

Have you ever tried this? *(Drink etc)*

Hey, we've met before, haven't we?

How about I buy you a drink?

Have you got your passport ready? We're off to Paris. *(Only for the rich.)*

# I:

I don't suppose you would be interested in going out one night to see a film?

I've been given a couple of tickets for the play/ concert on Thursday - do you want to come?

Isn't it boring here? Do you want to go somewhere else?

It's funny, but I'm sure I know you from somewhere.

I've got some news for you. *(When she asks you what it is, explain that you haven't got any news really, you just wanted an excuse to talk to her.)*

It's taken me half an hour to pluck up the courage to ask you for a drink. Please don't say no.

I don't normally do this sort of thing, but here's my card - I'd like too meet you some time.

I don't expect you to marry me, but will you at least have a drink with me?

It's my birthday - will you join me for a drink?

I know this will sound corny, but can I buy you a drink?

I've been trying to work out what to say to you for ages . . . that was it.

Is this seat taken?

# *J:*

Just a minute, don't I know you from somewhere?

Jingle bells, jingle bells . . . *(You're bound to meet some girls if you go carol singing)*

Just give me five minutes to chat you up, please.

# **K:**

Keep it up - you're doing well. *(Words of positive encouragement, useful if she is jogging, having a drinking competition, or pushing a car - make sure you help her with it.)*

Kiss me. *(For those of a bolder disposition.)*

# *L:*

Let me help you with that.

Listen, I want to tell you something . . .

Love your hair.

Let's get out of here. *(Useful if she looks bored and on her own.)*

Look, I've got to go. Is there any chance we can meet again?

Life has been empty without you. *(Careful with this one. Best used tongue-in-cheek.)*

# *M:*

Mine's a gin and tonic.

May I have the pleasure of this dance?

May I introduce myself?

Morning. How are you?

Maybe we could have a drink some time?

My friends said that you would definitely turn me down if I asked you for a drink. Help me prove them wrong.

# N:

Nobody I know can tell me who you are, but I'm sure I've seen you before.

No, don't tell me: you're a Pisces?

# O:

On a scale of one to ten, you have been voted ten by everyone over there. How do you feel?

Ooh, you don't wanna do that.

Oh dear, I told myself I would not fall in love tonight. You've just changed that.

Obviously this isn't very original, but can I get you something to drink?

# P:

Perhaps I've said this to you before, I can't remember, but you've got beautiful eyes.

Please take a seat.

Personally I feel that we could have a much better time somewhere else.

# Q:

Quite how you came to be so beautiful, I'll never know.

Queuing is so boring, don't you find?

Quick, the lights are coming back on in a minute. Kiss me.

# R:

Read my palm. What does it tell you? (*Opens up physical contact and gives her a chance to say what she really feels about you. This will either be that you are very sexy or that you like train spotting.*)

Ring me sometime. Must dash now, but here's my number.

Rather than stay here all evening, shall we go somewhere quieter?

# S:

Shall we share a taxi to the nightclub?

So what's your name?

Shall we introduce ourselves?

Shall we dance?

Some people can run a mile in four minutes, yet it took me half an hour to go the ten yards that have been separating us.

# T:

There's a party tonight. Do you want to come?

The trouble with this place is . . .

Tell me about yourself - you look interesting.

The music here is great/crap etc

# U:

Umpteen people must have already told you this, but you're very beautiful.

Um, hello.

Under this sophisticated, charming exterior lies a very shy person.

# V:

Virtually everyone here is ugly except you.

Very difficult getting served here. What are you having in case I get served first?

Very nice gear you've got on.

Visions of beauty are rare, but I think I've just seen one.

# W:

Would you like to dance? *(Not recommended for use on a train.)*

Weren't you at the party last week?

When I saw you I knew it was worth risking my male pride in order to talk to you, even if you ignore me.

Would you like some? *(If you are eating something and a girl is watching enviously.)*

Would you accept my last Rollo? *(Make sure you have one!)*

Where is the . . . ? *(Especially on holiday or away from your home town. Works best if you happen to know that she is going there too, so that you can walk with her and chat.)*

# X:

Xavia is an unusual name, but my name's . . .

# Y:

You show me yours, I'll show you mine.

You must tell me your name.

You probably think I'm mad coming up to you like this, but I have this strange urge to buy you a drink.

You must give me a chance to talk to you.

'Yes' is my favourite word. What's yours?

# Z:

Zoos are morally unacceptable, don't you think? *(If she is standing near a zoo holding a protest placard.)*

# Epilogue

To end this book I would like to summarise a few important points. Being single is the not the end of the world, the most important thing in life is to be happy. Remember that being in a relationship will not automatically bring happiness.

That said, relationships and playing the game of forming relationships can be a lot of fun. Whether you are meeting girls through dating agencies, mutual friends or as strangers in a pub, just try to be a 'nice person' to them, and strive for the ultimate balanced approach:

**Don't** be square but don't be so fashionable that everyone thinks you look stupid.

**Don't** force your attentions on her but don't be a wimp.

**Don't** excessively flatter her but don't insult her.

**Don't** have unpleasant body odour but don't wear so much aftershave that you smell like a perfume factory.

**Don't** talk about yourself all evening but don't be silent to the extent that it seems as if you have something to hide.

**Don't** be flashy but don't be dull.

**Don't** dismiss what she talks about as trivial but don't pander to every word she says like an obsequious servant.

**Don't** give up!

# Stop Looking

Aren't you tired of dates from Hell? Satisfy yourself with good times and good food. Along the way you'll meet new people over polo, tennis, theatre, horse racing, treasure hunts and even clay pigeon shooting! What happens after dinner is up to you. 081-741 1252 (London) 081-658 9441 (South East).

EST 6 YRS    *Dinner Dates*    6,000 MEMBERS

**For people who have too much on their plates to worry about their social life**

As featured on BBC's 'Food and Drink'

**AMERICANS**

Seek friendship
romance
and marriage
with British ladies
and gentlemen!
All ages!

English Rose / English Connection
(Dept SP),
24 Cecil Square,
Margate,
Kent,
CT9 1BA
Tel/Fax: (0843) 290735

*As featured on national television!*

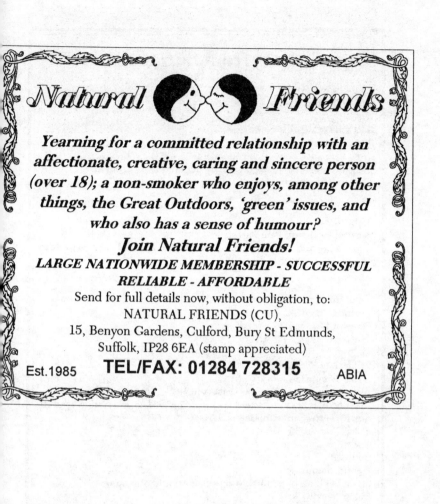

# *Natural* 👥 *Friends*

**Yearning for a committed relationship with an affectionate, creative, caring and sincere person (over 18); a non-smoker who enjoys, among other things, the Great Outdoors, 'green' issues, and who also has a sense of humour?**

### *Join Natural Friends!*

***LARGE NATIONWIDE MEMBERSHIP - SUCCESSFUL RELIABLE - AFFORDABLE***

Send for full details now, without obligation, to:
NATURAL FRIENDS (CU),
15, Benyon Gardens, Culford, Bury St Edmunds,
Suffolk, IP28 6EA (stamp appreciated)

Est.1985   **TEL/FAX: 01284 728315**   ABIA

# Other books from Summersdale:

*Classic Love Poems*
£10.99 (hardback)

*The Busker's Guide To Europe*
**Stewart Ferris**
How to make money from your talents
"A good practical handbook . . . buy this book and get out there"
**Guitarist Magazine**
£5.95

*Don't Lean Out Of The Window! Surviving Europe on a Train*
**Stewart Ferris and Paul Bassett**
Tongue-in-cheek travelogue about Inter Rail, as featured in **19 Magazine**
"Marvellous" **Stephen Fry**
£4.95

*From Horizontal To Vertical - Working With Paralysed People in Bangladesh*
**Corinna Thomas**
Foreword by the BBC's **Mark Tully**
£9.95

*Watch My Back - A Bouncer's Story*
**Geoff Thompson**
Autobiography of a bouncer - first volume.
"This book is ten years overdue - I read it in one go and couldn't put it down" **Terry Christian, Channel 4**
£12.99 (hardback)

*Bouncer*
**Geoff Thompson**
Second volume of mind-blowing autobiographical writing.
£14.99 (hardback)

*Real Self Defence*
**Geoff Thompson**
Illustrated self defence training manual for all levels.
£12.99

*The Pavement Arena*
*- Adapting Combat Martial Arts to the Street*
**Geoff Thompson**
£9.95

*The Student Grub Guide*
**Alastair Williams**
Favourite easy recipes for students.
£4.95

These titles are available from all good bookshops, but in case of difficulty send a cheque or postal order direct to SUMMERSDALE PUBLISHERS at the following address (add £1 p&p per book in UK, £3 per book overseas)
PO Box 49,
Chichester,
PO19 2FJ, UK
Allow up to 28 days for delivery.